POEMS ON
THE UNDERGROUND

POEMS

ON THE

UNDERGROUND

TENTH EDITION

EDITED BY

Gerard Benson · Judith Chernaik · Cicely Herbert

CASSELL

Cassell
Wellington House
125 Strand
London WC2R 0BB

Poems on the Underground first published
(as *100 Poems on the Underground*) 1991
This Tenth Edition published 2001

Reprinted 2002, 2004

British Library Cataloguing-in-Publication Data
A catalogue record for this book is available from the British Library

ISBN 0-304-35639-5

Printed and bound in Great Britain by
Mackays of Chatham plc, Chatham, Kent

www.orionbooks.co.uk

CONTENTS

List of Illustrations   *page* xxii
Preface to the Tenth Edition   xxiv
Introduction   xxv

THE POEMS   23

Up in the Morning Early   25
Robert Burns (1759–96)
Ozymandias   26
Percy Bysshe Shelley (1792–1822)
This Is Just to Say   27
William Carlos Williams (1883–1963)
The Railway Children   28
Seamus Heaney (b. 1939)
Like a Beacon   29
Grace Nichols (b. 1950)

Sonnet 29   30
William Shakespeare (1564–1616)
Her Anxiety   31
W. B. Yeats (1865–1939)
Lady 'Rogue' Singleton   32
Stevie Smith (1902–71)
The Trees   33
Philip Larkin (1922–85)
Benediction   34
James Berry (b. 1924)

The Sick Rose   35
William Blake (1757–1827)
'Much Madness is divinest Sense'   36
Emily Dickinson (1830–86)
At Lord's   37
Francis Thompson (1859–1907)
Rainforest   38
Judith Wright (1915–2000)
Encounter at St. Martin's   39
Ken Smith (1938–2003)

'Western wind when wilt thou blow'   40
Anon. (early 16th century)
Composed upon Westminster Bridge,
September 3, 1802   41
William Wordsworth (1770–1850)
Everyone Sang   42
Siegfried Sassoon (1886–1967)
The Loch Ness Monster's Song   43
Edwin Morgan (b. 1920)
Living   44
Denise Levertov (1923–97)

Holy Sonnet   45
('Death be not proud, though some have called thee')
John Donne (1572–1631)
'Trail all your pikes'   46
Anne Finch, Countess of Winchilsea (1661–1720)
Alas, Alack!   47
Walter de la Mare (1873–1956)
Immigrant   48
Fleur Adcock (b. 1934)
I Am Becoming My Mother   49
Lorna Goodison (b. 1947)

'Tagus farewell'   50
Sir Thomas Wyatt (1503–42)
Snow   51
Edward Thomas (1878–1917)
Lines *from* **Endymion**   53
John Keats (1795–1821)
Celia Celia   54
Adrian Mitchell (b. 1932)
Goodbye   54
Adrian Mitchell
Ragwort   55
Anne Stevenson (b. 1933)

'The silver swan'   56
Anon. (*c.* 1600)
'So we'll go no more a-roving'   57
George Gordon, Lord Byron (1788–1824)

Teeth   58
Spike Milligan (1918–2002)
To My First White Hairs   59
Wole Soyinka (b. 1935)
Riddle-Me-Ree   60
Liz Lochhead (b. 1947)

The Expulsion from Eden *from* **Paradise Lost,**
Book XII   61
John Milton (1608–74)
'There was an Old Man with a beard'   62
Edward Lear (1812–88)
Spring and Fall   63
Gerard Manley Hopkins (1844–89)
Dog Days   64
Derek Mahon (b. 1941)
The Visitor   65
Carolyn Forché (b. 1950)

Ariel's Song   66
William Shakespeare (1564–1616)
Meeting at Night   67
Robert Browning (1812–89)
Prelude I   68
T. S. Eliot (1888–1965)
London Airport   69
Christopher Logue (b. 1926)
Taid's Grave   70
Gillian Clarke (b. 1937)

The Coming of Grendel *from* **Beowulf**   71
(10th century or earlier)
translated by Gerard Benson
In my Craft or Sullen Art   72
Dylan Thomas (1914–53)
Midsummer, Tobago   73
Derek Walcott (b. 1930)
Sonnet from the Portuguese   75
('How do I love thee? Let me count the ways')
Elizabeth Barrett Browning (1806–61)

Handbag   76
Ruth Fainlight (b. 1931)

Symphony in Yellow   77
Oscar Wilde (1854–1900)
'Sumer is icumen in'   79
Anon. (13th century)
Song   80
('Stop all the clocks, cut off the telephone')
W. H. Auden (1907–73)
The Ancients of the World   81
R. S. Thomas (1913–2000)
Day Trip   82
Carole Satyamurti (b. 1939)

In Time of 'The Breaking of Nations'   83
Thomas Hardy (1840–1928)
London Bells   84
Anon. (early 18th century)
The Tyger   87
William Blake (1757–1827)
Delay   88
Elizabeth Jennings (1926–2001)
Everything Changes   89
Cicely Herbert (b. 1937)

Roundel *from* **The Parliament of Fowls**   90
Geoffrey Chaucer (1340?–1400)
Dreams   91
Robert Herrick (1591–1674)
Sonnet   92
('What lips my lips have kissed, and where, and why')
Edna St. Vincent Millay (1892–1950)
And Yet the Books   93
Czeslaw Milosz (1911–2004), *translated by* Czeslaw Milosz and
Robert Hass
The Leader   94
Roger McGough (b. 1937)

from **To the City of London**   95
William Dunbar (1465?–1530?)

On First Looking into Chapman's Homer 96
John Keats (1795–1821)
A Dead Statesman 97
Rudyard Kipling (1865–1936)
Modern Secrets 98
Shirley Geok-lin Lim (b. 1944)
Sergeant Brown's Parrot 99
Kit Wright (b. 1944)

'I have a gentil cock' 100
Anon. (early 15th century)
What Am I After All 101
Walt Whitman (1819–92)
Piano 102
D. H. Lawrence (1885–1930)
Mmenson 103
Kamau Brathwaite (b. 1930)
Light 104
Diane Wakoski (b. 1937)

from **The Song of Solomon** 105
The King James Bible (1611)
'You took away all the oceans and all the room' 106
Osip Mandelstam (1891–1938), *translated by* Clarence
Brown and W. S. Merwin
Wet Evening in April 107
Patrick Kavanagh (1906–67)
I Saw a Jolly Hunter 108
Charles Causley (1917–2003)
Aunt Jennifer's Tigers 109
Adrienne Rich (b. 1929)

Old English Riddle 110
Anon. (before 1000), *translated by* Gerard Benson
Virtue 111
George Herbert (1593–1633)
'I know the truth – give up all other truths!' 112
Marina Tsvetayeva (1892–1941), *translated by*
Elaine Feinstein
Love Without Hope 113
Robert Graves (1895–1985)

Full Moon and Little Frieda   114
Ted Hughes (1930–98)

'Since there's no help, come let us kiss and part'   115
Michael Drayton (1563–1631)
'Into my heart an air that kills'   116
A. E. Housman (1859–1936)
Dolor   117
Theodore Roethke (1908–63)
The Cries of London   118
Anon. (17th century)
A 14-Year-Old Convalescent Cat in the Winter   120
Gavin Ewart (1916–95)
Come. And Be My Baby   121
Maya Angelou (b. 1928)

'Ich am of Irlonde'   122
Anon. (14th century)
Song   123
('Now sleeps the crimson petal, now the white')
Alfred, Lord Tennyson (1809–92)
The Embankment   124
(The Fantasia of a Fallen Gentleman on a Cold, Bitter Night)
T. E. Hulme (1883–1917)
Stars and planets   125
Norman MacCaig (1910–96)
The Uncertainty of the Poet   126
Wendy Cope (b. 1945)

'I saw a Peacock with a fiery tail'   127
Anon. (17th century)
from **Frost at Midnight**   128
Samuel Taylor Coleridge (1772–1834)
Snow   129
Louis MacNeice (1907–63)
On Himself   130
David Wright (1920–94)
Sometimes   131
Sheenagh Pugh (b. 1950)

The Passionate Shepherd to his Love   132
Christopher Marlowe (1564–93)

Letter to André Billy. 9 April 1915 133
Guillaume Apollinaire (1880–1918), *translated by*
Oliver Bernard
Child 134
Sylvia Plath (1932–63)
A song for England 135
Andrew Salkey (1928–95)
Letters from Yorkshire 136
Maura Dooley (b. 1957)

The Bonnie Broukit Bairn 137
Hugh MacDiarmid (Christopher Murray Grieve)
(1892–1978)
To Emilia V– 139
Percy Bysshe Shelley (1792–1822)
Concerto for Double Bass 140
John Fuller (b. 1937)
Words, Wide Night 141
Carol Ann Duffy (b. 1955)
The Lobster Quadrille 142
Lewis Carroll (1832–98)

'I shall say what inordinate love is' 144
Anon. (15th century)
A red red Rose 145
Robert Burns (1759–96)
The Very Leaves of the Acacia-Tree are London 146
Kathleen Raine (1908–2003)
One Art 147
Elizabeth Bishop (1911–79)
To Someone Who Insisted I Look Up Someone 148
X. J. Kennedy (b. 1929)

Two Fragments 149
Sappho (fl. 600 BC), *translated by* Cicely Herbert
I Am 150
John Clare (1793–1864)
Dream Boogie 151
Langston Hughes (1902–67)
The Unpredicted 152
John Heath-Stubbs (b. 1918)

The Emigrant Irish   153
Eavan Boland (b. 1944)

from **The Garden**   154
Andrew Marvell (1621–78)
The Flaw in Paganism   155
Dorothy Parker (1893–1967)
Anthem for Doomed Youth   156
Wilfred Owen (1893–1918)
A Picture, *for Tiantian's fifth birthday*   158
Bei Dao (b. 1949), *translated by* Bonnie S. McDougall and
Chen Maiping
Idyll   160
U. A. Fanthorpe (b. 1929)

'Gray goose and gander'   161
Anon. (date unknown)
Sonnet: On His Blindness   162
John Milton (1608–74)
He wishes for the Cloths of Heaven   163
W. B. Yeats (1865–1939)
Late Summer Fires   164
Les Murray (b. 1938)
Love in a Bathtub   165
Sujata Bhatt (b. 1956)

The Twa Corbies   166
Anon. (before 1800)
'The Great Frost'   167
John Gay (1685–1732)
If I Could Tell You   168
W. H. Auden (1907–73)
Spacetime   169
Miroslav Holub (1923–98), *translated by* David Young and
Dana Hábová
Sun a-shine, rain a-fall   170
Valerie Bloom (b. 1956)

Sonnet 18   171
('Shall I compare thee to a summer's day?')
William Shakespeare (1564–1616)

A True and Faithful Inventory of the Goods 172
belonging to Dr. Swift
Thomas Sheridan (1687–1738)
Where Go the Boats? 173
Robert Louis Stevenson (1850–94)
Thanks Forever 174
Milton Kessler (1930–2000)
Swineherd 175
Eiléan Ní Chuilleanáin (b. 1942)

'The world is too much with us' 176
William Wordsworth (1770–1850)
A Birthday 178
Christina Rossetti (1830–94)
Disillusionment of Ten O'Clock 179
Wallace Stevens (1879–1955)
The Boundary Commission 180
Paul Muldoon (b. 1951)
Arrival 1946 181
Moniza Alvi (b. 1954)

'Now winter nights enlarge' 182
Thomas Campion (1567–1620)
'Let my shadow disappear into yours' ('Låt min
skugga försvinna i din') 183
Pär Lagerkvist (1891–1974), translated by W. H. Auden and
Leif Sjöberg
Do Not Go Gentle Into That Good Night 184
Dylan Thomas (1914–53)
Look at all those monkeys 185
Spike Milligan (1918–2002)
Mysteries 186
Dannie Abse (b. 1923)
Rooms 187
Kathleen Jamie (b. 1962)

The Good Morrow 188
John Donne (1572–1631)
Adlestrop 189
Edward Thomas (1878–1917)

from **Requiem** 190
Anna Akhmatova (1889–1966), *translated by*
Richard McKane
The Exiles 191
Iain Crichton Smith (1928–98)
Moonwise 192
Jean 'Binta' Breeze (b. 1956)

'My true love hath my heart and I have his' 193
Sir Philip Sidney (1554–86)
Acquainted with the Night 194
Robert Frost (1874–1963)
from **Summoned by Bells** 195
John Betjeman (1906–84)
A Glass of Water 196
May Sarton (1912–95)
Wind 197
James Fenton (b. 1949)

To My Dear and Loving Husband 198
Anne Bradstreet (1612–72)
Chorus from a Play 199
John Dryden (1631–1700)
Inversnaid 200
Gerard Manley Hopkins (1844–89)
Saturday Morning 201
Hugo Williams (b. 1942)
The Undertaking 202
Louise Glück (b. 1943)

His Return to London 203
Robert Herrick (1591–1674)
'I taste a liquor never brewed' 204
Emily Dickinson (1830–86)
The Poet 205
George Mackay Brown (1921–96)
Greenwich Park 206
Herbert Lomas (b. 1924)
Apology 207
Mimi Khalvati (b. 1944)

'Under the greenwood tree'   208
William Shakespeare (1564–1616)
from **Poetry** (La poesía)   209
Pablo Neruda (1904–73), *translated by*
Alastair Reid
Memory of my Father   210
Patrick Kavanagh (1906–67)
Secret Lives   211
Siân Hughes
Potosí   212
Pauline Stainer
The Lesson (an anti-pastoral)   213
Tracy Ryan

'**My lefe ys faren in a lond**'   214
Anon. (15th century)
from **Ecclesiastes**   216
The King James Bible (1611)
Nightsong: City   217
Dennis Brutus (b. 1924)
Shopper   218
Connie Bensley (b. 1929)
The Rescue   219
Seamus Heaney (b. 1939)

Rondel   220
Charles d'Orléans (1394–1465), *translated by*
Oliver Bernard
from **An Essay on Man**   221
Alexander Pope (1688–1744)
The Faun (Le Faune)   223
Paul Verlaine (1844–96), *translated by*
John Montague
Cargoes   224
John Masefield (1878–1967)
Waiting for Rain in Devon   225
Peter Porter (b. 1929)
Wedding   226
Alice Oswald (b. 1966)

from **Mutabilitie**   227
Edmund Spenser (1552–99)

Harvestwoman (Ceifeira)   229
Fernando Pessoa (1888–1935), *translated by*
Jonathan Griffin
Expectans Expectavi   230
Anne Ridler (1912–2001)
Mama Dot   231
Fred D'Aguiar (b. 1960)
Voyage to the Bottom of the Sea   232
Stephen Knight (b. 1960)

Sic Vita   233
Henry King (1592–1669)
from **Dover Beach**   234
Matthew Arnold (1822–88)
The Reassurance   235
Thom Gunn (1929–2004)
Don't Call Alligator Long-Mouth till You Cross River   236
John Agard (b. 1949)
The Language Issue   237
Nuala Ní Dhomhnaill (b. 1952), *translated from the Irish*
by Paul Muldoon

EUROPEAN POEMS ON THE UNDERGROUND
(*see note* page 348)

Longings (Επιθυμίες)   238
C. P. Cavafy (1863–1933), *translated by*
Edmund Keeley and Philip Sherrard
Hope (Förhoppning)   239
Edith Södergran (1892–1923), *translated by*
Herbert Lomas
Peaceful Waters: Variation (Remansos: Variación)   241
Federico García Lorca (1898–1936), *translated by*
Adrian Mitchell
'Fresh sighs for sale!' ('Achetez mes soupirs')   242
Alain Bosquet (1919–98), *translated by*
Samuel Beckett
25 February 1944 (25 febbraio 1944)   243
Primo Levi (1919–87), *translated by*
Eleonora Chiavetta

25 April 1974 (25 de Abril)   244
Sophia de Mello Breyner (b. 1919), *translated by*
Ruth Fainlight
A Collector (Ein Sammler)   245
Erich Fried (1921–88), *translated by*
Stuart Hood
'Somewhere in the house' ('Ergens in huis')   246
Hanny Michaelis (b. 1922), *translated by*
Marjolijn de Jager
Distances (Les distances)   247
Philippe Jaccottet (b. 1925), *translated by*
Derek Mahon
The birds will still sing (Les oiseaux continuent
à chanter)   248
Anise Koltz (b. 1928), *translated by*
John Montague
$a$capitalist$ (et%kapitalistisk%)   249
Vagn Steen (b. 1928), *translated by*
the poet
From March '79 (Från Mars-79)   250
Tomas Tranströmer (b. 1931), *translated by*
John F. Deane
Merlin   251
Geoffrey Hill (b. 1932)
This Moment   252
Eavan Boland (b. 1944)

The Gateway   253
A. D. Hope (1907–2000)
'I sing of a maiden'   255
Anon. (early 15th century)
'Thread suns' ('Fadensonnen')   256
Paul Celan (1920–70), *translated by*
Michael Hamburger

Song, *to Celia*   257
Ben Jonson (1572–1637)
Father William   258
Lewis Carroll (1832–98)
Home-Thoughts, from Abroad   260
Robert Browning (1812–89)

Fenland Station in Winter   261
Katherine Pierpoint (b. 1961)
Monopoly   262
Paul Farley (b. 1965)

Caedmon's Hymn   263
(7th century AD), *translated by* Paul Muldoon
Anglo-Saxon Riddle   264
Anon. (before 1000), *translated by* Kevin Crossley-Holland
from **The General Prologue to The Canterbury Tale**s   265
Geoffrey Chaucer (1340?–1400)
Sonnet 116   266
('Let me not to the marriage of true minds')
William Shakespeare (1564–1616)
The Argument of His Book   267
Robert Herrick (1591–1674)
Jerusalem   268
William Blake (1757–1827)

'I would to heaven that I were so much clay'   269
George Gordon, Lord Byron (1788–1824)
from **Among School Children**   270
W. B. Yeats (1865–1939)
Not Waving but Drowning   271
Stevie Smith (1902–71)
Map of the New World: Archipelagoes   272
Derek Walcott (b. 1930)
After the Fall   273
Anne Stevenson (b. 1933)
Quark   274
Jo Shapcott (b. 1953)

'Loving the rituals'   275
Palladas (4th century AD), *translated by* Tony Harrison
Auld Lang Syne   276
Robert Burns (1759–96)
from **St. Paul's Epistle to the Corinthians**   278
translated by William Tyndale (1484–1536)
from **Lines written a few miles above Tintern Abbey**   279
William Wordsworth (1770–1850)
from **In Memoriam**   280
Alfred, Lord Tennyson (1809–92)

'There came a Wind like a Bugle'   281
Emily Dickinson (1830–86)
First Fig   282
Edna St. Vincent Millay (1892–1950)
Song   283
Elizabeth Bishop (1911–79)
Naima, *for John Coltrane*   284
Kamau Brathwaite (b. 1930)
Season   285
Wole Soyinka (b. 1935)
Prayer   286
Carol Ann Duffy (b. 1955)

Season Song   287
Anon. (9th century), *translated by*
Flann O'Brien
'No man is an island'   288
John Donne (1572–1631)
A Song   289
Laetitia Pilkington (1708–50)
Chorus from Hellas   290
Percy Bysshe Shelley (1792–1822)
Return to Cornwall   291
Charles Causley (1917–2003)
True Stories (1)   292
Margaret Atwood (b. 1939)
Guinep   293
Olive Senior (b. 1943)
Road   294
Don Paterson (b. 1963)

from **Beowulf**   295
Anon. (10th century or earlier), *translated by*
Seamus Heaney
For Pero Moniz, who died at sea   296
Luís de Camões (1524–80), *English version by*
Paul Hyland
Cradle Song   298
Thomas Dekker (1570–1632)
Eternity   299
William Blake (1757–1827)

The Catch   300
Simon Armitage (b. 1963)

AUSTRALIAN POEMS ON THE UNDERGROUND

Sunrise Sequence, *translated by*   301
Ronald M. Berndt
Mountain   302
Judith Wright (1915–2000)
Nasturtium Scanned   303
Judith Rodriguez (b. 1936)

from **The Vision of Piers Plowman**   304
William Langland (*c.* 1332–1400)
'Fear no more the heat o' the sun'   305
William Shakespeare (1564–1616)
Sea Love   306
Charlotte Mew (1869–1928)
To My Daughter   307
Stephen Spender (1909–95)
Thaw   308
David Malouf (b. 1934)
Epilogue   309
Grace Nichols (b. 1950)

YOUNG POETS ON THE UNDERGROUND

Night Caller   310
Lucy Pogson
The Flags   311
Matthew Paskins
I Think My Brain Is Coming Out of My Ears   312
Luke Yates

from **The World**   313
Henry Vaughan (1621–95)
A Riddle   314
Anon. (18th century)
February – not everywhere   315
Norman MacCaig (1910–96)
Peace (after Goethe)   316
David Constantine (b. 1944)

The Present   317
Michael Donaghy (b. 1954)
Seed   318
Paula Meehan (b. 1955)

What He Said   319
Cempulappeyanirar (1st–3rd century AD), *translated by*
A. K. Ramanujan
The Maiden's Song   320
Anon. (16th century)
On a General Election   322
Hilaire Belloc (1870–1953)
from **The Mind Is An Ancient and Famous Capital**   323
Delmore Schwartz (1913–66)
Misty   324
Ruth Padel (b. 1947)
A Private Life   325
John Burnside (b. 1955)

Sonnet 73   326
William Shakespeare (1564–1616)
Grass   327
Carl Sandburg (1878–1967)
The Sunflower   328
('Portami il girasole')
Eugenio Montale (1889–1981), *English version by* Jeremy Reed
The Sunburst   329
Michael Longley (b. 1939)
Freight song   330
Judith Kazantzis (b. 1940)

Notes to the Poems   331

Acknowledgements   354

Index of Poets and Translators   364

Index of First Lines   368

A Note of Thanks   377

LIST OF ILLUSTRATIONS

1	'Westron wynde when wylt thou blow'	*page* 40
2	Alas, Alack!	47
3	'Tagus farewell'	50
4	Endymion	52
5	'The silver Swanne'	56
6	Teeth	58
7	'There was an Old Man with a beard'	62
8	Ariel	66
9	'How do I love thee?'	74
10	Caricature of Oscar Wilde in a Top Hat	77
11	'Sumer is icumen in'	78
12	London Bells	85
13	The Tyger	86
14	Introduction to *The Parliament of Fowls*	90
15	To the City of London	95
16	Sergeant Brown's Parrot	99
17	I Saw a Jolly Hunter	108
18	Old English Riddle	110
19	The Cries of London. Setting by Orlando Gibbons	119
20	'Music, when soft voices die'	138
21	The Lobster Quadrille	143
22	'I shall say what inordinate love is'	144
23	The Algonquin Round Table	155
24	Anthem for Doomed Youth	157
25	A Picture (calligraphy)	159
26	Sun a-shine, rain a-fall	170
27	Where Go the Boats?	173
28	'The world is too much with us'	177
29	Look at all those monkeys	185
30	Summoned by Bells	195
31	'My lefe ys faren in a lond'	215
32	Le Faune	222
33	Fernando Pessoa	228

34 'Lunar Pierrot'   240
35 'I sing of a maiden' and 'I have a gentil cock'   254
36 Father William   259
37 Caedmon's Hymn   263
38 Self-portrait of Stevie Smith   271
39 Guinep   293
40 A Riddle   314
41 Traditional Tamil design   319
42 The Maiden's Song   321

PREFACE TO THE 10TH EDITION

IT IS fifteen years since we launched the first set of Poems on the Underground. We hardly imagined then what a hold on the public imagination our idea was to have. Five years later, Cassell published *100 Poems on the Underground*, which instantly became a poetry bestseller, and the anthology has been updated each year since then.

This tenth edition of the anthology contains over 300 poems from continents and cultures as diverse as the people who travel London's Underground system. We can still hardly believe our good fortune: from the beginning the project has been a voyage of discovery, excitement and pure pleasure for us and, it seems, for the millions of readers who have been able to share our enthusiasms and our sometimes quirky choices.

Each new set of poems can be found on the Poetry Society's website (www.poetrysoc.com), along with further information on the project: workshops, readings and concerts of poetry and music. London Underground's website (www.thetube.com) also features the poems. Following our two-year celebration of 'A Thousand Years of Poetry in English', special projects have included a set of poems by Australian writers, new translations of poems by Camões and Goethe, and a display of poems by young poets, winners of the Poetry Society's annual competition. Poems from our collection have also appeared on all 7,500 London buses.

All the poems reprinted here have been displayed in London Underground trains, and the posters have been sent to schools and libraries throughout the UK. Old and new poems sit easily together in the great democratic meeting-place that is the London Underground – a most hospitable, if unexpected, venue for the imaginative life. We continue to receive support, encouragement and suggestions for poems from a large readership, to whom we say: long may poetry flourish on the Underground, on the printed page, and in the hearts and minds of the people.

Gerard Benson, Judith Chernaik, Cicely Herbert
LONDON, 2001

INTRODUCTION

ANYONE who suffers from an addiction to reading cereal box tops will understand the special appeal of Poems on the Underground. The programme began as an idea shared among a few friends; how pleasant it would be, we thought, to read a few lines by a favourite poet on the Tube, instead of advertisements for package holidays. We were Londoners by birth or adoption, users of public transport, lovers of poetry. We shared the conviction that poetry is a popular, living art, and that the pleasures of rhythm and rhyme are part of common life. The Underground had large numbers of empty advertising spaces. It seemed reasonable to propose filling the blank grey slots with poems, for the entertainment of the travelling public.

London Underground was surprisingly responsive to our suggestion that they provide spaces free for this civic purpose. They agreed that if we could raise money to pay for 500 spaces, they would match the number. With an Arts Council grant from a fund set up 'for the wider dissemination of poetry', and support from the publishers Faber and Faber and Oxford University Press, we presented the first group of poems to an unsuspecting public.

On a rain-drenched January morning, Poems on the Underground was officially launched at Aldwych, a station (now defunct) used for filming movies about the Second World War. Many of those who descended to the Underground platform that morning might have had in mind the journey made to the infernal regions by Orpheus in search of Eurydice. Ordinary signs – 'THIS WAY DOWN', 'STAND CLEAR', 'DOORS CLOSING' – assume special significance when such a setting is taken over by poets and their friends. Official party fare was coffee and doughnuts, but wine flowed too, and when the train bearing its consignment of poems arrived twenty minutes late, we all climbed aboard, pursued by representatives of the press, radio and television. Within minutes the carriages were alive to the sounds of happy poets declaiming their verses, interspersed with lines by Shelley and Keats.

When we began to scatter poems about in public, we had no idea how people would respond. It was a bit reminiscent of the lovesick youth in the Forest of Arden, hanging 'odes upon haw-thorns and elegies on brambles'. Not that the London Under-ground is anything like the Forest of Arden; on the contrary, it is the ultimate expression of the urban working world. But poetry thrives on paradox, and the poems seemed to take on new life when they were removed from books and set among the adverts. Commuters enjoyed the idea of reading Keats's 'Much have I travell'd in the realms of gold' on a crowded Central Line train, or trying to memorise a sonnet between Leicester Square and Hammersmith. Just as we had hoped, the poems provided relief, caused smiles, offered refreshment to the soul – and all in a place where one would least expect to find anything remotely poetic.

The truth, as we soon discovered, is that Britain is a nation of poetry lovers. Hundreds of people wrote in with queries about particular poems and suggestions of their own; many letters just said, in effect, 'Thank you, whoever you are, for the poems'. Three years after our launch, London Underground agreed to provide all spaces free and to quadruple the number, providing at least one poem to each train carriage. Posters go to over a hundred British Council libraries abroad, and the Poetry Society maintains a sub-scription list, mainly for schools and libraries, but also for hospi-tals, community centres and prisons. We seem set to continue indefinitely, with no possibility of running out of poems short enough to amuse or console a huge captive readership.

From the start, we have tried to offer as wide a variety of tone and subject matter as possible, to share our own favourites and discoveries, and also to present new voices. At least two poems out of each group of six are by living poets. We have taken material from the earliest times to the present, and we have made a point of including poets from English-speaking countries throughout the world. Translations are also included (some of them specially commissioned by us), and 'Anon.' features in songs and riddles, nursery rhymes and broadside ballads.

We have kept a special place for London poems and poets who had close ties with London – Donne, Milton, Blake, Keats and the Brownings, among others – though some well-known London poems, such as 'To the City of London' by the Scottish poet William Dunbar and Wordsworth's 'Composed Upon Westminster Bridge', were written by poets as they were passing through. Of

London poems by contemporary writers, one is by Fleur Adcock, born in New Zealand, another by the Guyanese-born Grace Nichols. Then again, A. E. Housman wrote *A Shropshire Lad* when he was Professor of Latin at University College London; and we have assumed that the imagination is free to wander where it will. What we have listened for is the individual voice, and we have tried to offer poems in which the poet's voice speaks directly to the modern reader about the common themes of poetry through the ages.

The great subjects are well represented here: love, death, war, exile, the natural world, time, memory. But these are not the only themes of poetry, nor is the high-flown the only mode. We have included writers of comic nonsense like Edward Lear, Spike Milligan and Wendy Cope; there are also pieces in a witty, conversational vein by Michael Drayton and William Carlos Williams, Stevie Smith and Liz Lochhead. Some light verse was chosen with children in mind, but we found that these poems appealed as much to adults as to children; Roger McGough's 'The Leader' found its way into boardrooms and political party headquarters, as well as public transport systems in Vienna and Moscow.

For, strange as it seems, poems on trains and buses are now part of the urban landscape in cities across the world, from Paris to St. Petersburg, Shanghai to Melbourne. Many schemes have been inspired by our example, starting with Dublin's 'Poems on the Dart' – posters in green ink on the coastal railway, with station names evoking the ghosts of Yeats, Joyce and Beckett. We have also 'exchanged' poems with public transport systems in Stockholm and Helsinki, and with New York's 'Poetry in Motion', when poems by Rita Dove and Thom Gunn displaced train announcements at Grand Central Station during the cheerful launch party.

In London, interest in the Tube poems and poets has led to poetry readings at the British Library, the Barbican, the South Bank, the National Portrait Gallery and London's Transport Museum. We've also given writing workshops for adults and children in schools, libraries and more unlikely places, including, one chill September dawn, Westminster Bridge.

The close links between poetry and song have inspired several commissions for performance with the Apollo Chamber Orchestra: new poems for Saint-Saëns' *Carnival of the Animals*; musical settings of poems by W. H. Auden and Maya Angelou; and a rock score by Sally Herbert of *Goblin Market*, by Christina Rossetti. Our popular Conway Hall concerts with the Apollo Chamber Orchestra and guest poets are represented in our first CD for Meridian Records, featuring Jim Parker's settings of Sir John Betjeman's London poems and Oscar Wilde's 'Symphony in Yellow'.

This anthology has come about in response to public interest in the programme, and in particular poems that appeared briefly on the Tube and then vanished from sight, leaving only a memory of a single line or image. They are all here (with one substitution) in the order in which they appeared on the Tube. Many poems will be familiar to readers; others are fairly obscure and hard to find without special library resources; some are unique to this volume. We hope that the collection as a whole will appeal not only to confirmed poetry lovers but also to readers who are coming to poetry for the first time.

THE POEMS

Up in the Morning Early

Cauld blaws the wind frae east to west,
   The drift is driving sairly;
Sae loud and shrill's I hear the blast,
   I'm sure it's winter fairly.

CHORUS: Up in the morning's no for me,
   Up in the morning early;
When a' the hills are cover'd wi' snaw,
   I'm sure it's winter fairly.

The birds sit chittering in the thorn,
   A' day they fare but sparely;
And lang's the night frae e'en to morn,
   I'm sure it's winter fairly.

CHORUS: Up in the morning's no for me,
   Up in the morning early;
When a' the hills are cover'd wi' snaw,
   I'm sure it's winter fairly.

ROBERT BURNS (1759–96)

Ozymandias

I met a traveller from an antique land
Who said: Two vast and trunkless legs of stone
Stand in the desert . . . Near them, on the sand,
Half sunk, a shattered visage lies, whose frown,
And wrinkled lip, and sneer of cold command,
Tell that its sculptor well those passions read
Which yet survive, stamped on these lifeless things,
The hand that mocked them and the heart that fed;
And on the pedestal these words appear:
"My name is OZYMANDIAS, king of kings:
Look on my works, ye Mighty, and despair!"
Nothing beside remains. Round the decay
Of that colossal wreck, boundless and bare
The lone and level sands stretch far away.

PERCY BYSSHE SHELLEY (1792–1822)

This Is Just to Say

I have eaten
the plums
that were in
the icebox

and which
you were probably
saving
for breakfast

Forgive me
they were delicious
so sweet
and so cold

WILLIAM CARLOS WILLIAMS (1883–1963)

The Railway Children

When we climbed the slopes of the cutting
We were eye-level with the white cups
Of the telegraph poles and the sizzling wires.

Like lovely freehand they curved for miles
East and miles west beyond us, sagging
Under their burden of swallows.

We were small and thought we knew nothing
Worth knowing. We thought words travelled the wires
In the shiny pouches of raindrops,

Each one seeded full with the light
Of the sky, the gleam of the lines, and ourselves
So infinitesimally scaled

We could stream through the eye of a needle.

SEAMUS HEANEY (b. 1939)

Like a Beacon

In London
every now and then
I get this craving
for my mother's food
I leave art galleries
in search of plantains
saltfish/sweet potatoes

I need this link

I need this touch
of home
swinging my bag
like a beacon
against the cold

GRACE NICHOLS (b. 1950)

Sonnet 29

When in disgrace with Fortune and men's eyes,
I all alone beweep my outcast state,
And trouble deaf heaven with my bootless cries,
And look upon myself and curse my fate,
Wishing me like to one more rich in hope,
Featured like him, like him with friends possessed,
Desiring this man's art, and that man's scope,
With what I most enjoy contented least,
Yet in these thoughts myself almost despising,
Haply I think on thee, and then my state
(Like to the lark at break of day arising
From sullen earth) sings hymns at heaven's gate,
    For thy sweet love remembered such wealth brings,
    That then I scorn to change my state with kings.

WILLIAM SHAKESPEARE (1564–1616)

Her Anxiety

Earth in beauty dressed
Awaits returning spring.
All true love must die,
Alter at the best
Into some lesser thing.
Prove that I lie.

Such body lovers have,
Such exacting breath,
That they touch or sigh.
Every touch they give,
Love is nearer death.
Prove that I lie.

W. B. YEATS (1865–1939)

Lady 'Rogue' Singleton

Come, wed me, Lady Singleton,
And we will have a baby soon
And we will live in Edmonton
Where all the friendly people run.

I could never make you happy, darling,
Or give you the baby you want,
I would always very much rather, dear,
Live in a tent.

I am not a cold woman, Henry,
But I do not feel for you,
What I feel for the elephants and the miasmas
And the general view.

STEVIE SMITH (1902–71)

The Trees

The trees are coming into leaf
Like something almost being said;
The recent buds relax and spread,
Their greenness is a kind of grief.

Is it that they are born again
And we grow old? No, they die too.
Their yearly trick of looking new
Is written down in rings of grain.

Yet still the unresting castles thresh
In fullgrown thickness every May.
Last year is dead, they seem to say,
Begin afresh, afresh, afresh.

PHILIP LARKIN (1922–85)

Benediction

Thanks to the ear
that someone may hear

Thanks to seeing
that someone may see

Thanks to feeling
that someone may feel

Thanks to touch
that one may be touched

Thanks to flowering of white moon
and spreading shawl of black night
holding villages and cities together

JAMES BERRY (b. 1924)

The Sick Rose

O Rose thou art sick.
The invisible worm
That flies in the night
In the howling storm,

Has found out thy bed
Of crimson joy:
And his dark secret love
Does thy life destroy.

WILLIAM BLAKE (1757–1827)

'Much Madness is divinest Sense'

Much Madness is divinest Sense –
To a discerning Eye –
Much Sense – the starkest Madness –
'Tis the Majority
In this, as All, prevail –
Assent – and you are sane –
Demur – you're straightway dangerous –
And handled with a Chain –

EMILY DICKINSON (1830–86)

At Lord's

It is little I repair to the matches of the Southron folk,
   Though my own red roses there may blow;
It is little I repair to the matches of the Southron folk,
   Though the red roses crest the caps, I know.
For the field is full of shades as I near the shadowy coast,
And a ghostly batsman plays to the bowling of a ghost,
And I look through my tears on a soundless-clapping host
   As the run-stealers flicker to and fro,
       To and fro: –
 O my Hornby and my Barlow long ago!

FRANCIS THOMPSON (1859–1907)

Rainforest

The forest drips and glows with green.
The tree-frog croaks his far-off song.
His voice is stillness, moss and rain
drunk from the forest ages long.

We cannot understand that call
unless we move into his dream,
where all is one and one is all
and frog and python are the same.

We with our quick dividing eyes
measure, distinguish and are gone.
The forest burns, the tree-frog dies,
yet one is all and all are one.

JUDITH WRIGHT (1915–2000)

Encounter at St. Martin's

I tell a wanderer's tale, the same
I began long ago, a boy in a barn,
I am always lost in it. The place
is always strange to me. In my pocket

the wrong money or none, the wrong paper,
maps of another town, the phrase book
for yesterday's language, just a ticket
to the next station, and my instructions.

In the lobby of the Banco Bilbao
a dark woman will slip me a key, a package,
the name of a hotel, a numbered account,
the first letters of an unknown alphabet.

KEN SMITH (1938–2003)

'Western wind when wilt thou blow'

Western wind when wilt thou blow
the small rain down can rain
Christ if my love were in my arms
and I in my bed again

ANON. (early 16th century)

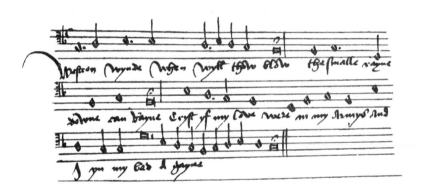

'Westron wynde when wylt thou blow'   Musical setting in a tenor part-book, dating from the early 16th century, which provides the only known source of this famous lyric. BL Royal MS, Appendix 58, f.5. By permission of The British Library Board.

Composed upon Westminster Bridge, September 3, 1802

Earth has not anything to show more fair:
Dull would he be of soul who could pass by
A sight so touching in its majesty:
This City now doth like a garment wear
The beauty of the morning; silent, bare,
Ships, towers, domes, theatres, and temples lie
Open unto the fields, and to the sky;
All bright and glittering in the smokeless air.
Never did sun more beautifully steep
In his first splendour valley, rock, or hill;
Ne'er saw I, never felt, a calm so deep!
The river glideth at his own sweet will:
Dear God! the very houses seem asleep;
And all that mighty heart is lying still!

WILLIAM WORDSWORTH (1770–1850)

Everyone Sang

Everyone suddenly burst out singing;
And I was filled with such delight
As prisoned birds must find in freedom,
Winging wildly across the white
Orchards and dark-green fields; on – on – and out of sight.

Everyone's voice was suddenly lifted;
And beauty came like the setting sun:
My heart was shaken with tears; and horror
Drifted away . . . O, but Everyone
Was a bird; and the song was wordless; the singing will
   never be done.

April 1919

SIEGFRIED SASSOON (1886–1967)

The Loch Ness Monster's Song

Sssnnnwhuffffll?
Hnwhuffl hhnnwfl hnfl hfl?
Gdroblboblhobngbl gbl gl g g g g glbgl.
Drublhaflablhaflubhafgabhaflhafl fl fl –
gm grawwwww grf grawf awfgm graw gm.
Hovoplodok-doplodovok-plovodokot-doplodokosh?
Splgraw fok fok splgrafhatchgabrlgabrl fok splfok!
Zgra kra gka fok!
Grof grawff gahf?
Gombl mbl bl –
blm plm,
blm plm,
blm plm,
blp.

EDWIN MORGAN (b. 1920)

Living

The fire in leaf and grass
so green it seems
each summer the last summer.

The wind blowing, the leaves
shivering in the sun,
each day the last day.

A red salamander
so cold and so
easy to catch, dreamily

moves his delicate feet
and long tail. I hold
my hand open for him to go.

Each minute the last minute.

DENISE LEVERTOV (1923–97)

Holy Sonnet

Death be not proud, though some have called thee
Mighty and dreadful, for thou art not so;
For those whom thou think'st thou dost overthrow
Die not, poor death, nor yet canst thou kill me.
From rest and sleep, which but thy pictures be,
Much pleasure, then from thee much more must flow;
And soonest our best men with thee do go,
Rest of their bones, and souls' delivery.
Thou art slave to Fate, chance, kings, and desperate men,
And dost with poison, war, and sickness dwell,
And poppy or charms can make us sleep as well,
And better than thy stroke; why swell'st thou then?
One short sleep past, we wake eternally,
And death shall be no more, Death thou shalt die.

JOHN DONNE (1572–1631)

'Trail all your pikes'

Trail all your pikes, dispirit every drum,
March in a slow procession from afar,
Ye silent, ye dejected men of war!
Be still the hautboys, and the flute be dumb!
Display no more, in vain, the lofty banner.
For see! where on the bier before ye lies
The pale, the fall'n, th'untimely sacrifice
To your mistaken shrine, to your false idol Honour!
from ALL IS VANITY

ANNE FINCH, Countess of Winchilsea (1661–1720)

Alas, Alack!

Ann, Ann!
　　Come! quick as you can!
There's a fish that *talks*
　　In the frying-pan.
Out of the fat,
　　As clear as glass,
He put up his mouth
　　And moaned 'Alas!'
Oh, most mournful,
　　'Alas, alack!'
Then turned to his sizzling,
　　And sank him back.

WALTER DE LA MARE (1873–1956)

Alas, Alack!　Drawing by W. Heath Robinson, © The Estate of
Mrs J. C. Robinson. By permission of Laurence Pollinger.

Immigrant

November '63: eight months in London.
I pause on the low bridge to watch the pelicans:
they float swanlike, arching their white necks
over only slightly ruffled bundles of wings,
burying awkward beaks in the lake's water.

I clench cold fists in my Marks and Spencer's jacket
and secretly test my accent once again:
St James's Park; St James's Park; St James's Park.

FLEUR ADCOCK (b. 1934)

I Am Becoming My Mother

Yellow/brown woman
fingers smelling always of onions

My mother raises rare blooms
and waters them with tea
her birth waters sang like rivers
my mother is now me

My mother had a linen dress
the colour of the sky
and stored lace and damask
tablecloths
to pull shame out of her eye.

I am becoming my mother
brown/yellow woman
fingers smelling always of onions.

LORNA GOODISON (b. 1947)

'Tagus farewell'

Tagus farewell, that westward with thy streams
Turns up the grains of gold already tried:
With spur and sail for I go seek the Thames
Gainward the sun that showeth her wealthy pride
And to the town which Brutus sought by dreams
Like bended moon doth lend her lusty side.
My king, my country, alone for whom I live,
Of mighty love the wings for this me give.

SIR THOMAS WYATT (1503–42)

'Tagus farewell'   A rare example of a poem in the author's hand, in a
handsome leatherbound notebook he kept from 1537 to 1542, which contains
over one hundred poems by Wyatt and several by the Earl of Surrey, most of
them in the hand of an amanuensis. The notebook was also used for drafts of
letters and mathematical computations over a period of one hundred years.
BL Egerton 2711, f.69. By permission of The British Library Board.

Snow

In the gloom of whiteness,
In the great silence of snow,
A child was sighing
And bitterly saying: 'Oh,
They have killed a white bird up there on her nest,
The down is fluttering from her breast!'
And still it fell through that dusky brightness
On the child crying for the bird of the snow.

EDWARD THOMAS (1878–1917)

Endymion Book 1st

A thing of beauty is a joy for ever:
Its loveliness increases; it will never
Pass into nothingness; but still will keep
A Bower quiet for us, and a sleep
Full of sweet dreams, and health, and quiet breathing.
Therefore, on every morrow, are we wreathing
A flowery band to bind us to the earth,
Spite of Despondence, & of the inhuman dearth
Of noble natures of the gloomy days,
Of all the unhealthy and oer-darkened ways
Made for our searching: yes, in spite of all
Some shape of beauty moves away the Pall
From our dark Spirits, and before us dances
Like glitter on the points of Latian's lances,

Endymion   The opening lines of the autograph fair copy, with Keats's corrections.
MA 208. By permission of The Pierpont Morgan Library, New York.

Lines *from* Endymion

A thing of beauty is a joy for ever:
Its loveliness increases; it will never
Pass into nothingness; but still will keep
A bower quiet for us, and a sleep
Full of sweet dreams, and health, and quiet breathing.
Therefore, on every morrow, are we wreathing
A flowery band to bind us to the earth,
Spite of despondence, of the inhuman dearth
Of noble natures, of the gloomy days,
Of all the unhealthy and o'er-darkened ways
Made for our searching: yes, in spite of all,
Some shape of beauty moves away the pall
From our dark spirits.

JOHN KEATS (1795–1821)

Celia Celia

When I am sad and weary
When I think all hope has gone
When I walk along High Holborn
I think of you with nothing on

ADRIAN MITCHELL (b. 1932)

Goodbye

He breathed in air, he breathed out light.
Charlie Parker was my delight.

ADRIAN MITCHELL

Ragwort

They won't let railways alone, those yellow flowers.
They're that remorseless joy of dereliction
darkest banks exhale like vivid breath
as bricks divide to let them root between.
How every falling place concocts their smile,
taking what's left and making a song of it.

ANNE STEVENSON (b. 1933)

'The silver swan'

The silver swan, who living had no note,
When death approached unlocked her silent throat,
Leaning her breast against the reedy shore,
Thus sung her first and last, and sung no more:
Farewell all joys, O death come close mine eyes,
More geese than swans now live, more fools than wise.

ANON. (*c.* 1600)

'The silver Swanne'   A setting by the court composer Orlando Gibbons of this anonymous elegiac poem, in *The First Set of Madrigals and Mottets* (1612). It has been suggested that the poem may refer to the death of Edmund Spenser, in 1599. BL Royal Mus. 15.e.2 (10). By permission of The British Library Board.

'So we'll go no more a-roving'

So we'll go no more a-roving
　So late into the night,
Though the heart be still as loving,
　And the moon be still as bright.

For the sword outwears its sheath,
　And the soul wears out the breast,
And the heart must pause to breathe,
　And Love itself have rest.

Though the night was made for loving,
　And the day returns too soon,
Yet we'll go no more a-roving
　By the light of the moon.

GEORGE GORDON, LORD BYRON (1788–1824)

Teeth

English Teeth, English Teeth!
Shining in the sun
A part of British heritage
Aye, each and every one.

English Teeth, Happy Teeth!
Always having fun
Clamping down on bits of fish
And sausages half done.

English Teeth! HEROES' Teeth!
Hear them click! and clack!
Let's sing a song of praise to them –
Three Cheers for the Brown Grey and Black.

SPIKE MILLIGAN (1918–2002)

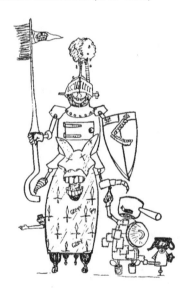

Teeth   Drawing by the author, in *Silly Verse for Kids* © Spike Milligan,
by permission of Spike Milligan Productions.

To My First White Hairs

Hirsute hell chimney-spouts, black thunderthroes
confluence of coarse cloudfleeces – my head sir! – scourbrush
in bitumen, past fossil beyond fingers of light – until . . . !

Sudden sprung as corn stalk after rain, watered milk weak;
as lightning shrunk to ant's antenna, shrivelled
off the febrile sight of crickets in the sun –

THREE WHITE HAIRS! frail invaders of the undergrowth
interpret time. I view them, wired wisps, vibrant coiled
beneath a magnifying glass, milk-thread presages

Of the hoary phase. Weave then, weave o quickly weave
your sham veneration. Knit me webs of winter sagehood,
nightcap, and the fungoid sequins of a crown.

WOLE SOYINKA (b. 1935)

Riddle-Me-Ree

My first is in life (not contained within heart)
My second's in whole but never in part.
My third's in forever, but also in vain.
My last's in ending, why not in pain?

is love the answer?

LIZ LOCHHEAD (b. 1947)

The Expulsion from Eden

In either hand the hast'ning angel caught
Our ling'ring parents, and to th' eastern gate
Led them direct, and down the cliff as fast
To the subjected plain; then disappeared.
They looking back, all th' eastern side beheld
Of Paradise, so late their happy seat,
Waved over by that flaming brand, the gate
With dreadful faces thronged and fiery arms:
Some natural tears they dropped, but wiped them soon;
The world was all before them, where to choose
Their place of rest, and Providence their guide:
They hand in hand with wand'ring steps and slow,
Through Eden took their solitary way.

from PARADISE LOST, BOOK XII

JOHN MILTON (1608–74)

'There was an Old Man with a beard'

There was an Old Man with a beard,
Who said, "It is just as I feared! –
    Two Owls and a Hen,
    Four Larks and a Wren,
Have all built their nests in my beard!"
    from THE BOOK OF NONSENSE

EDWARD LEAR (1812–88)

'There was an Old Man with a beard'   Drawing by the author, from
The Book of Nonsense.

Spring and Fall

to a young child

Margaret, are you grieving
Over Goldengrove unleaving?
Leaves, like the things of man, you
With your fresh thoughts care for, can you?
Ah! as the heart grows older
It will come to such sights colder
By and by, nor spare a sigh
Though worlds of wanwood leafmeal lie;
And yet you *will* weep and know why.
Now no matter, child, the name:
Sorrow's springs are the same.
Nor mouth had, no nor mind, expressed
What heart heard of, ghost guessed:
It is the blight man was born for,
It is Margaret you mourn for.

GERARD MANLEY HOPKINS (1844–89)

Dog Days

'When you stop to consider
The days spent dreaming of a future
And say then, that was my life.'

For the days are long –
From the first milk van
To the last shout in the night,
An eternity. But the weeks go by
Like birds; and the years, the years
Fly past anti-clockwise
Like clock hands in a bar mirror.

DEREK MAHON (b. 1941)

The Visitor

In Spanish he whispers there is no time left.
It is the sound of scythes arcing in wheat,
the ache of some field song in Salvador.
The wind along the prison, cautious
as Francisco's hands on the inside, touching
the walls as he walks, it is his wife's breath
slipping into his cell each night while he
imagines his hand to be hers. It is a small country.

There is nothing one man will not do to another.

CAROLYN FORCHÉ (b. 1950)

Ariel's Song

Full fathom five thy father lies,
  Of his bones are coral made:
Those are pearls that were his eyes,
  Nothing of him that doth fade,
But doth suffer a sea-change
Into something rich, and strange:
Sea-nymphs hourly ring his knell –
  Hark! now I hear them,
    Ding-dong bell.

from THE TEMPEST

WILLIAM SHAKESPEARE (1564–1616)

Ariel Illustration by Arthur Rackham.

Meeting at Night

The grey sea and the long black land;
And the yellow half-moon large and low;
And the startled little waves that leap
In fiery ringlets from their sleep,
As I gain the cove with pushing prow,
And quench its speed i' the slushy sand.

Then a mile of warm sea-scented beach;
Three fields to cross till a farm appears;
A tap at the pane, the quick sharp scratch
And blue spurt of a lighted match,
And a voice less loud, thro' its joys and fears,
Than the two hearts beating each to each!

ROBERT BROWNING (1812–89)

Prelude I

The winter evening settles down
With smell of steaks in passageways.
Six o'clock.
The burnt-out ends of smoky days.
And now a gusty shower wraps
The grimy scraps
Of withered leaves about your feet
And newspapers from vacant lots;
The showers beat
On broken blinds and chimney-pots,
And at the corner of the street
A lonely cab-horse steams and stamps.

And then the lighting of the lamps.

T. S. ELIOT (1888–1965)

London Airport

Last night in London Airport
I saw a wooden bin
labelled UNWANTED LITERATURE
IS TO BE PLACED HEREIN.
So I wrote a poem
and popped it in.

CHRISTOPHER LOGUE (b. 1926)

Taid's Grave

Rain on lilac leaves. In the dusk
they show me the grave,
a casket of stars underfoot,
his name there, and his language.

Voice of thrushes in rain.
My cousin Gwynfor eases me
into the green cave.
Wet hands of lilac

touch my wrist and the secret
unfreckled underside of my arm
daring fingers to count
five warm blue eggs.

GILLIAN CLARKE (b. 1937)

Taid: Welsh for grandfather

The Coming of Grendel

Now from the marshlands under the mist-mountains
Came Grendel prowling; branded with God's ire.
This murderous monster was minded to entrap
Some hapless human in that high hall.
On he came under the clouds, until clearly
He could see the great golden feasting place,
Glimmering wine-hall of men. Not his first
Raid was this on the homeplace of Hrothgar.
Never before though and never afterward
Did he encounter hardier defenders of a hall.

from BEOWULF (10th century or earlier)

translated by GERARD BENSON

In my Craft or Sullen Art

In my craft or sullen art
Exercised in the still night
When only the moon rages
And the lovers lie abed
With all their griefs in their arms,
I labour by singing light
Not for ambition or bread
Or the strut and trade of charms
On the ivory stages
But for the common wages
Of their most secret heart.

Not for the proud man apart
From the raging moon I write
On these spindrift pages
Nor for the towering dead
With their nightingales and psalms
But for the lovers, their arms
Round the griefs of the ages,
Who pay no praise or wages
Nor heed my craft or art.

DYLAN THOMAS (1914–53)

Midsummer, Tobago

Broad sun-stoned beaches.

White heat.
A green river.

A bridge,
scorched yellow palms

from the summer-sleeping house
drowsing through August.

Days I have held,
days I have lost,

days that outgrow, like daughters,
my harbouring arms.

DEREK WALCOTT (b. 1930)

XLIII

How do I love thee ? Let me count the ways !
I love thee to the depth & breadth & height
My soul can reach, when feeling out of sight
For the ends of Being and ideal Grace .
I love thee to the level of everyday's
Most quiet need, by sun & candlelight .
I love thee freely, as men strive for Right ;
I love thee purely, as they turn from Praise .
I love thee with the passion put to use
In my old griefs ; and with my childhood's faith .
I love thee with the love I seemed to lose
With my lost Saints ! I love thee with the breath
Smiles, tears, of all my life — and, if God choose,
I shall but love thee better after death .

'How do I love thee?'   Autograph manuscript, with corrections, of one of the most popular 'Sonnets from the Portuguese'. BL Add. MS 43487, f.49. By permission of The British Library Board.

Sonnet from the Portuguese

How do I love thee? Let me count the ways.
I love thee to the depth and breadth and height
My soul can reach, when feeling out of sight
For the ends of Being and ideal Grace.
I love thee to the level of everyday's
Most quiet need, by sun and candlelight.
I love thee freely, as men strive for Right;
I love thee purely, as they turn from Praise.
I love thee with the passion put to use
In my old griefs, and with my childhood's faith.
I love thee with a love I seemed to lose
With my lost saints, – I love thee with the breath,
Smiles, tears, of all my life! – and, if God choose,
I shall but love thee better after death.

ELIZABETH BARRETT BROWNING (1806–61)

Handbag

My mother's old leather handbag,
crowded with letters she carried
all through the war. The smell
of my mother's handbag: mints
and lipstick and Coty powder.
The look of those letters, softened
and worn at the edges, opened,
read, and refolded so often.
Letters from my father. Odour
of leather and powder, which ever
since then has meant womanliness,
and love, and anguish, and war.

RUTH FAINLIGHT (b. 1931)

Symphony in Yellow

An omnibus across the bridge
  Crawls like a yellow butterfly,
  And, here and there, a passer-by
Shows like a little restless midge.

Big barges full of yellow hay
  Are moored against the shadowy wharf,
  And, like a yellow silken scarf,
The thick fog hangs along the quay.

The yellow leaves begin to fade
  And flutter from the Temple elms,
  And at my feet the pale green Thames
Lies like a rod of rippled jade.

OSCAR WILDE (1854–1900)

Caricature of Oscar Wilde in a Top Hat Black and white drawing by Beatrice Whistler. Birnie Philip Bequest. By permission of The Hunterian Art Gallery, University of Glasgow.

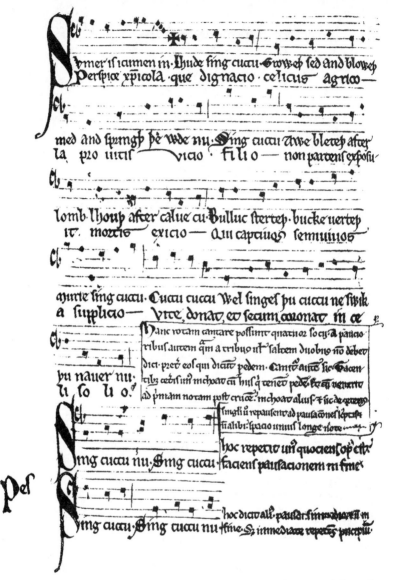

'Sumer is icumen in' English and Latin texts, with music, of the earliest known English round. The Latin text is completely unrelated to the English original. From a manuscript transcribed at Reading Abbey in the early 13th century. BL Harley 978. f.11v. By permission of The British Library Board.

'Sumer is icumen in'

Sumer is icumen in,
Loud sing cuckoo!
Groweth seed and bloweth mead
And springeth the wood now.
Sing cuckoo!

Ewe bleateth after lamb,
Cow loweth after calf,
Bullock starteth, buck farteth,
Merry sing cuckoo!

Cuckoo, cuckoo!
Well singest thou cuckoo,
Nor cease thou never now!

Sing cuckoo now, sing cuckoo!
Sing cuckoo, sing cuckoo now!

ANON. (13th century)

Song

Stop all the clocks, cut off the telephone,
Prevent the dog from barking with a juicy bone,
Silence the pianos and with muffled drum
Bring out the coffin, let the mourners come.

Let aeroplanes circle moaning overhead
Scribbling on the sky the message He Is Dead,
Put crêpe bows round the white necks of the public doves,
Let the traffic policemen wear black cotton gloves.

He was my North, my South, my East and West,
My working week and my Sunday rest,
My noon, my midnight, my talk, my song;
I thought that love would last for ever: I was wrong.

The stars are not wanted now; put out every one,
Pack up the moon and dismantle the sun,
Pour away the ocean and sweep up the wood;
For nothing now can ever come to any good.

W. H. AUDEN (1907–73)

The Ancients of the World

The salmon lying in the depths of Llyn Llifon,
   Secretly as a thought in a dark mind,
Is not so old as the owl of Cwm Cowlyd
   Who tells her sorrow nightly on the wind.

The ousel singing in the woods of Cilgwri,
   Tirelessly as a stream over the mossed stones,
Is not so old as the toad of Cors Fochno
   Who feels the cold skin sagging round his bones.

The toad and the ousel and the stag of Rhedynfre,
   That has cropped each leaf from the tree of life,
Are not so old as the owl of Cwm Cowlyd,
   That the proud eagle would have to wife.

R. S. THOMAS (1913–2000)

Day Trip

Two women, seventies, hold hands
on the edge of Essex,
hair in strong nets,
shrieked laughter echoing gulls
as shingle sucks from under feet
easing in brine.

There must be an unspoken point
when the sea feels like
their future. No longer paddling,
ankles submerge in lace,
in satin ripple.
Dress hems darken.

They do not risk their balance
for the shimmering of ships
at the horizon's sweep
as, thigh deep, they inch on
fingers splayed, wrists bent,
learning to walk again.

CAROLE SATYAMURTI (b. 1939)

In Time of 'The Breaking of Nations'

I

Only a man harrowing clods
  In a slow silent walk
With an old horse that stumbles and nods
  Half asleep as they stalk.

II

Only thin smoke without flame
  From the heaps of couch-grass;
Yet this will go onward the same
  Though Dynasties pass.

III

Yonder a maid and her wight
  Come whispering by:
War's annals will cloud into night
  Ere their story die.

THOMAS HARDY (1840–1928)

'Thou art my battle axe and weapons of war: for with thee will I break in pieces the nations, and with thee will I destroy kingdoms' (Jeremiah: 51.20).

London Bells

Two sticks and an apple,
Ring the bells at Whitechapel.

Old Father Bald Pate,
Ring the bells Aldgate.

Maids in white aprons,
Ring the bells at St. Catherine's.

Oranges and lemons,
Ring the bells at St. Clement's.

When will you pay me?
Ring the bells at the Old Bailey.

When I am rich,
Ring the bells at Fleetditch.

When will that be?
Ring the bells at Stepney.

When I am old,
Ring the great bell at Paul's.

ANON. (early 18th century)

London Bells.

Two Sticks & an Apple,
Ring y̌ Bells at Whitechapple
Old Father Bald Pate,
Ring y̌ Bells Aldgate,
Maids in white Aprons,
Ring y̌ Bells a S.ᵗ Cathrines,
Oranges

Oranges and Lemmons,
Ring y̌ Bells at S.ᵗ Clemens,
When will you pay me,
Ring y̌ Bells at y̌ OldBailey
When I am Rich,
Ring y̌ Bells at Fleet ditch,
When will that be,
Ring y̌ Bells at Stepney,
When I am Old,
Ring y̌ great Bell at Pauls.

London Bells   The traditional London rhyme as it appears in an early hand-set printed children's book, *Tommy Thumb's Pretty Song Book* (1744), Vol. II. By permission of The British Library Board.

The Tyger   A much-corrected autograph draft of the poem, in Blake's notebook, the 'Rossetti Manuscript'. BL Add. MS 49460, f.56. By permission of The British Library Board.

The Tyger

Tyger Tyger, burning bright,
In the forests of the night;
What immortal hand or eye,
Could frame thy fearful symmetry?

In what distant deeps or skies
Burnt the fire of thine eyes!
On what wings dare he aspire?
What the hand, dare sieze the fire?

And what shoulder, & what art,
Could twist the sinews of thy heart?
And when thy heart began to beat,
What dread hand? & what dread feet?

What the hammer? what the chain?
In what furnace was thy brain?
What the anvil? what dread grasp,
Dare its deadly terrors clasp?

When the stars threw down their spears
And water'd heaven with their tears:
Did he smile his work to see?
Did he who made the Lamb make thee?

Tyger Tyger, burning bright,
In the forests of the night:
What immortal hand or eye,
Dare frame thy fearful symmetry?

WILLIAM BLAKE (1757–1827)

Delay

The radiance of that star that leans on me
Was shining years ago. The light that now
Glitters up there my eye may never see,
And so the time lag teases me with how

Love that loves now may not reach me until
Its first desire is spent. The star's impulse
Must wait for eyes to claim it beautiful
And love arrived may find us somewhere else.

ELIZABETH JENNINGS (1926–2001)

Everything Changes

after Brecht, *'Alles wandelt sich'*

Everything changes. We plant
trees for those born later
but what's happened has happened,
and poisons poured into the seas
cannot be drained out again.

What's happened has happened.
Poisons poured into the seas
cannot be drained out again, but
everything changes. We plant
trees for those born later.

CICELY HERBERT (b. 1937)

Roundel

Now welcome Summer with thy sunnè soft,
That hast this winter's weathers overshake,
And driven away the longè nightès black.

Saint Valentine, that art full high aloft,
Thus singen smallè fowlès for thy sake:
Now welcome Summer with thy sunnè soft,
That hast this winter's weathers overshake.

Well have they cause for to gladden oft,
Since each of them recovered hath his make.
Full blissful may they singè when they wake:
Now welcome Summer with thy sunnè soft,
That hast this winter's weathers overshake,
And driven away the longè nightès black!

from THE PARLIAMENT OF FOWLS

GEOFFREY CHAUCER (1340?–1400)

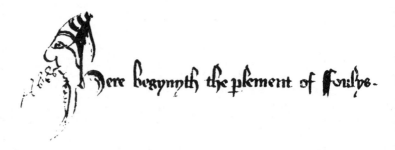

Introduction to *The Parliament of Fowls* from a 15th-century copy of Chaucer's *Works* in the Cambridge University Library. GG.4.27, f.480b. By permission of the Syndics of Cambridge University Library.

Dreams

Here we are all, by day; by night we're hurled
By dreams, each one, into a several world.

ROBERT HERRICK (1591–1674)

Sonnet

What lips my lips have kissed, and where, and why,
I have forgotten, and what arms have lain
Under my head till morning; but the rain
Is full of ghosts tonight, that tap and sigh
Upon the glass and listen for reply,
And in my heart there stirs a quiet pain
For unremembered lads that not again
Will turn to me at midnight with a cry.
Thus in the winter stands the lonely tree,
Nor knows what birds have vanished one by one,
Yet knows its boughs more silent than before:
I cannot say what loves have come and gone,
I only know that summer sang in me
A little while, that in me sings no more.

EDNA ST. VINCENT MILLAY (1892–1950)

And Yet the Books

And yet the books will be there on the shelves, separate beings,
That appeared once, still wet
As shining chestnuts under a tree in autumn,
And, touched, coddled, began to live
In spite of fires on the horizon, castles blown up,
Tribes on the march, planets in motion.
"We are," they said, even as their pages
Were being torn out, or a buzzing flame
Licked away their letters. So much more durable
Than we are, whose frail warmth
Cools down with memory, disperses, perishes.
I imagine the earth when I am no more:
Nothing happens, no loss, it's still a strange pageant,
Women's dresses, dewy lilacs, a song in the valley.
Yet the books will be there on the shelves, well born,
Derived from people, but also from radiance, heights.

CZESLAW MILOSZ (1911–2004)

translated by CZESLAW MILOSZ *and* ROBERT HASS

The Leader

I wanna be the leader
I wanna be the leader
Can I be the leader?
Can I? I can?
Promise? Promise?
Yippee, I'm the leader
I'm the leader

OK what shall we do?

ROGER McGOUGH (b. 1937)

from To the City of London

Above all rivers thy river hath renown,
Whose beryl streamės, pleasant and preclare,
Under thy lusty wallės runneth down;
Where many a swan doth swim with wingės fair,
Where many a barge doth sail, and row with oar,
Where many a ship doth rest with top-royal.
O town of townės, patron and not compare,
London, thou art the flower of Cities all.

WILLIAM DUNBAR (1465?–1530?)

To the City of London   The 'river' stanza. The full text of the poem is
copied into *The Chronicle of London 1215–1509*, where the poem is said to have
been 'made' while the company was sitting at dinner. BL Cotton MS Vitell.
A.XVI, f.200v. By permission of The British Library Board.

On First Looking into Chapman's Homer

Much have I travell'd in the realms of gold,
   And many goodly states and kingdoms seen;
   Round many western islands have I been
Which bards in fealty to Apollo hold.
Oft of one wide expanse had I been told
   That deep-brow'd Homer ruled as his demesne;
   Yet did I never breathe its pure serene
Till I heard Chapman speak out loud and bold:
Then felt I like some watcher of the skies
   When a new planet swims into his ken;
Or like stout Cortez when with eagle eyes
   He star'd at the Pacific – and all his men
Look'd at each other with a wild surmise –
   Silent, upon a peak in Darien.

JOHN KEATS (1795–1821)

A Dead Statesman

I could not dig: I dared not rob:
Therefore I lied to please the mob.
Now all my lies are proved untrue
And I must face the men I slew.
What tale shall serve me here among
Mine angry and defrauded young?

from EPITAPHS OF THE WAR 1914–18

RUDYARD KIPLING (1865–1936)

Modern Secrets

Last night I dreamt in Chinese.
Eating Yankee shredded wheat
I said it in English
To a friend who answered
In monosyllables:
All of which I understood.

The dream shrank to its fiction.
I had understood its end
Many years ago. The sallow child
Ate rice from its ricebowl
And hides still in the cupboard
With the china and tea-leaves.

SHIRLEY GEOK-LIN LIM (b. 1944)

Sergeant Brown's Parrot

Many policemen wear upon their shoulders
Cunning little radios. To pass away the time
They talk about the traffic to them, listen to the news,
And it helps them to Keep Down Crime.

But Sergeant Brown, he wears upon his shoulder
A tall green parrot as he's walking up and down
And all the parrot says is "Who's-a-pretty-boy-then?"
"I am," says Sergeant Brown.

KIT WRIGHT (b. 1944)

Sergeant Brown's Parrot   Drawing by Posy Simmonds, © Posy
Simmonds. By permission of Collins Publishers.

'I have a gentil cock'

I have a gentil cock
  croweth me day
he doth me risen early
  my matins for to say

I have a gentil cock
  comen he is of great
his comb is of red coral
  his tail is of jet

I have a gentil cock
  comen he is of kind
his comb is of red sorrel
  his tail is of inde

his legs be of azure
  so gentil and so small
his spurs are of silver white
  into the wortewale

his eyes are of crystal
  locked all in amber
and every night he percheth him
  in my lady's chamber

ANON. (early 15th century)

What Am I After All

What am I after all but a child, pleas'd with the sound of
      my own name? repeating it over and over;
I stand apart to hear – it never tires me.

To you your name also;
Did you think there was nothing but two or three
      pronunciations in the sound of your name?

WALT WHITMAN (1819–92)

Piano

Softly, in the dusk, a woman is singing to me;
Taking me back down the vista of years, till I see
A child sitting under the piano, in the boom of the tingling
    strings
And pressing the small, poised feet of a mother who smiles
    as she sings.

In spite of myself, the insidious mastery of song
Betrays me back, till the heart of me weeps to belong
To the old Sunday evenings at home, with winter outside
And hymns in the cosy parlour, the tinkling piano our guide.

So now it is vain for the singer to burst into clamour
With the great black piano appassionato. The glamour
Of childish days is upon me, my manhood is cast
Down in the flood of remembrance, I weep like a child for
    the past.

D. H. LAWRENCE (1885–1930)

Mmenson

Summon now the kings of the forest,
horn of the elephant,
mournful call of the elephant;

summon the emirs, kings of the desert,
horses caparisoned, beaten gold bent,
archers and criers, porcupine arrows, bows bent;

recount now the gains and the losses:
Agades, Sokoto, El Hassan dead in his tent,
the silks and the brasses, the slow weary tent

of our journeys down slopes, dry river courses;
land of the lion, land of the leopard, elephant
country; tall grasses, thick prickly herbs. Blow elephant

trumpet; summon the horses,
dead horses, our losses: the bent
slow bow of the Congo, the watering Niger . . .

KAMAU BRATHWAITE (b. 1930)

Light

I live for books
and light to read them in.
                              Waterlilies
reaching up
from the depths of the pond
algae dark,
the frog loves a jell of
blue-green water,
                    the bud
scales
a rope of stem,
then floats in sunshine. Like soap
in the morning bath.
This book I read
floats in my hand like a waterlily
coming out of the nutrient waters
of thought
and light shines on us both,
the morning's breviary.

DIANE WAKOSKI (b. 1937)

from **The Song of Solomon**

My beloved spake, and said unto me, Rise up, my love, my fair
    one, and come away.
For lo, the winter is past, the rain is over, and gone.
The flowers appear on the earth, the time of the singing of
    birds is come, and the voice of the turtle is heard in our
    land.
The fig tree putteth forth her green figs, and the vines with
    the tender grape give a good smell.
Arise, my love, my fair one, and come away.

THE KING JAMES BIBLE (1611)

'You took away all the oceans and all the room'

You took away all the oceans and all the room.
You gave me my shoe-size in earth with bars around it.
Where did it get you? Nowhere.
You left me my lips, and they shape words, even in silence.

OSIP MANDELSTAM (1891–1938)
translated by CLARENCE BROWN *and* W. S. MERWIN

Wet Evening in April

The birds sang in the wet trees
And as I listened to them it was a hundred years from now
And I was dead and someone else was listening to them.
But I was glad I had recorded for him
   The melancholy.

PATRICK KAVANAGH (1906–67)

I Saw a Jolly Hunter

I saw a jolly hunter
　With a jolly gun
Walking in the country
　In the jolly sun.

In the jolly meadow
　Sat a jolly hare.
Saw the jolly hunter.
　Took jolly care.

Hunter jolly eager –
　Sight of jolly prey.
Forgot gun pointing
　Wrong jolly way.

Jolly hunter jolly head
　Over heels gone.
Jolly old safety catch
　Not jolly on.

Bang went the jolly gun.
　Hunter jolly dead.
Jolly hare got clean away.
　Jolly good, I said.

CHARLES CAUSLEY (1917–2003)

I Saw a Jolly Hunter　Drawing by
Pat Marriott, from *Figgie Hobbin*.
By permission of Macmillan London.

Aunt Jennifer's Tigers

Aunt Jennifer's tigers prance across a screen,
Bright topaz denizens of a world of green.
They do not fear the men beneath the tree;
They pace in sleek chivalric certainty.

Aunt Jennifer's fingers fluttering through her wool
Find even the ivory needle hard to pull.
The massive weight of Uncle's wedding band
Sits heavily upon Aunt Jennifer's hand.

When Aunt is dead, her terrified hands will lie
Still ringed with ordeals she was mastered by.
The tigers in the panel that she made
Will go on prancing, proud and unafraid.

ADRIENNE RICH (b. 1929)

Old English Riddle

A moth, I thought, munching a word.
How marvellously weird! a worm
Digesting a man's sayings –
A sneakthief nibbling in the shadows
At the shape of a poet's thunderous phrases –
How unutterably strange!
And the pilfering parasite none the wiser
For the words he has swallowed.

from THE EXETER BOOK

ANON. (*before* 1000)
translated by GERARD BENSON

Answer: Bookworm

Old English Riddle From *The Exeter Book*, a manuscript of about the year 1000, containing over ninety riddles and several other Old English poems. Reprinted with the permission of the Dean and Chapter of Exeter Cathedral.

Virtue

Sweet day, so cool, so calm, so bright,
The bridal of the earth and sky:
The dew shall weep thy fall tonight;
                    For thou must die.

Sweet rose, whose hue angry and brave
Bids the rash gazer wipe his eye:
Thy root is ever in its grave,
                    And thou must die.

Sweet spring, full of sweet days and roses,
A box where sweets compacted lie;
My music shows ye have your closes,
                    And all must die.

Only a sweet and virtuous soul,
Like seasoned timber, never gives;
But though the whole world turn to coal,
                    Then chiefly lives.

GEORGE HERBERT (1593–1633)

'I know the truth – give up all other truths!'

I know the truth – give up all other truths!
No need for people anywhere on earth to struggle.
Look – it is evening, look, it is nearly night:
what do you speak of, poets, lovers, generals?

The wind is level now, the earth is wet with dew,
the storm of stars in the sky will turn to quiet.
And soon all of us will sleep under the earth, we
who never let each other sleep above it.

1915

MARINA TSVETAYEVA (1892–1941)
translated by ELAINE FEINSTEIN

Love Without Hope

Love without hope, as when the young bird-catcher
Swept off his tall hat to the Squire's own daughter,
So let the imprisoned larks escape and fly
Singing about her head, as she rode by.

ROBERT GRAVES (1895–1985)

Full Moon and Little Frieda

A cool small evening shrunk to a dog bark and the clank
of a bucket –

And you listening.
A spider's web, tense for the dew's touch.
A pail lifted, still and brimming – mirror
To tempt a first star to a tremor.

Cows are going home in the lane there, looping the hedges
with their warm wreaths of breath –
A dark river of blood, many boulders,
Balancing unspilled milk.

'Moon!' you cry suddenly, 'Moon! Moon!'

The moon has stepped back like an artist gazing amazed
at a work
That points at him amazed.

TED HUGHES (1930–98)

'Since there's no help, come let us kiss and part'

Since there's no help, come let us kiss and part,
Nay, I have done: you get no more of me,
And I am glad, yea glad with all my heart
That thus so cleanly I myself can free,
Shake hands forever, cancel all our vows,
And when we meet at any time again,
Be it not seen in either of our brows
That we one jot of former love retain.
Now at the last gasp of love's latest breath,
When his pulse failing, passion speechless lies,
When faith is kneeling by his bed of death,
And innocence is closing up his eyes,
    Now if thou wouldst, when all have given him over,
    From death to life thou mightst him yet recover.

MICHAEL DRAYTON (1563–1631)

'Into my heart an air that kills'

Into my heart an air that kills
   From yon far country blows:
What are those blue remembered hills,
   What spires, what farms are those?

That is the land of lost content,
   I see it shining plain,
The happy highways where I went
   And cannot come again.

from A SHROPSHIRE LAD

A. E. HOUSMAN (1859–1936)

Dolor

I have known the inexorable sadness of pencils,
Neat in their boxes, dolor of pad and paper-weight,
All the misery of manilla folders and mucilage,
Desolation in immaculate public places,
Lonely reception room, lavatory, switchboard,
The unalterable pathos of basin and pitcher,
Ritual of multigraph, paper-clip, comma,
Endless duplication of lives and objects.
And I have seen dust from the walls of institutions,
Finer than flour, alive, more dangerous than silica,
Sift, almost invisible, through long afternoons of tedium,
Dropping a fine film on nails and delicate eyebrows,
Glazing the pale hair, the duplicate grey standard faces.

THEODORE ROETHKE (1908–63)

The Cries of London

Here's fine rosemary, sage, and thyme.
Come buy my ground ivy.
Here's fetherfew, gilliflowers and rue.
Come buy my knotted marjorum, ho!
Come buy my mint, my fine green mint.
Here's fine lavender for your cloaths.
Here's parsley and winter-savory,
And hearts-ease, which all do choose.
Here's balm and hissop, and cinquefoil,
All fine herbs, it is well known.
    Let none despise the merry, merry cries
    Of famous London-town!

Here's fine herrings, eight a groat.
Hot codlins, pies and tarts.
New mackerel! have to sell.
Come buy my Wellfleet oysters, ho!
Come buy my whitings fine and new.
Wives, shall I mend your husbands horns?
I'll grind your knives to please your wives,
And very nicely cut your corns.
Maids, have you any hair to sell,
Either flaxen, black, or brown?
    Let none despise the merry, merry cries
    Of famous London-town!

ANON. (17th century)

The Cries of London   A setting by Orlando Gibbons of several London
'Cries' for five singers and five viol players. BL. Add.MS 29373, f.33v.
By permission of The British Library Board.

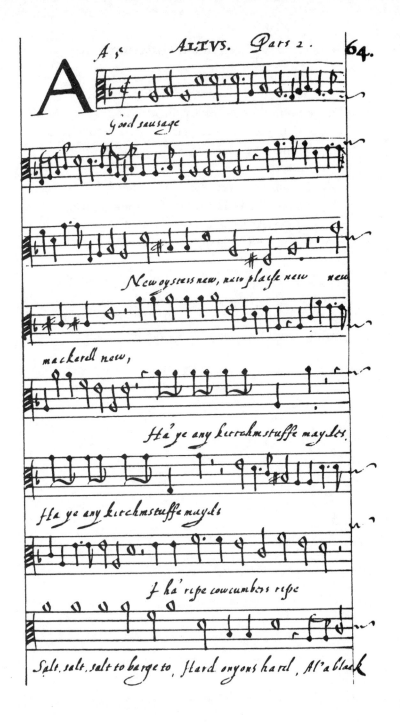

A 5

Good sausage

New oysters new, new place new   new

mackerell new,

Ha' ye any kitchmstuffe maydes

Ha ye any kitchmstuffe mayds

I ha' ripe cowcumbers ripe

Salt. salt. salt to barge to, Mard onyons haud, Al'a black

A 14-Year-Old Convalescent Cat in the Winter

I want him to have another living summer,
to lie in the sun and enjoy the *douceur de vivre* –
because the sun, like golden rum in a rummer,
is what makes an idle cat *un tout petit peu ivre* –

I want him to lie stretched out, contented,
revelling in the heat, his fur all dry and warm,
an Old Age Pensioner, retired, resented
by no one, and happinesses in a beelike swarm

to settle on him – postponed for another season
that last fated hateful journey to the vet
from which there is no return (and age the reason),
which must soon come – as I cannot forget.

GAVIN EWART (1916–95)

Come. And Be My Baby

The highway is full of big cars
going nowhere fast
And folks is smoking anything that'll burn
Some people wrap their lives around a cocktail glass
And you sit wondering
where you're going to turn.
I got it.
Come. And be my baby.

Some prophets say the world is gonna end tomorrow
But others say we've got a week or two
The paper is full of every kind of blooming horror
And you sit wondering
what you're gonna do.
I got it.
Come. And be my baby.

MAYA ANGELOU (b. 1928)

'Ich am of Irlonde'

I am of Ireland,
And of the holy land
Of Ireland.

Good sir, pray I thee,
For of saint charity,
Come and dance with me
In Ireland.

ANON. (14th century)

Song

Now sleeps the crimson petal, now the white;
Nor waves the cypress in the palace walk;
Nor winks the gold fin in the porphyry font:
The fire-fly wakens: waken thou with me.

Now droops the milkwhite peacock like a ghost,
And like a ghost she glimmers on to me.

Now lies the Earth all Danaë to the stars,
And all thy heart lies open unto me.

Now slides the silent meteor on, and leaves
A shining furrow, as thy thoughts in me.

Now folds the lily all her sweetness up,
And slips into the bosom of the lake:
So fold thyself, my dearest, thou, and slip
Into my bosom and be lost in me.

from THE PRINCESS

ALFRED, LORD TENNYSON (1809–92)

The Embankment

*(The Fantasia of a Fallen Gentleman on a Cold,
Bitter Night)*

Once, in finesse of fiddles found I ecstasy,
In a flash of gold heels on the hard pavement.
Now see I
That warmth's the very stuff of poesy.
Oh, God, make small
The old star-eaten blanket of the sky,
That I may fold it round me and in comfort lie.

T. E. HULME (1883–1917)

Stars and planets

Trees are cages for them: water holds its breath
To balance them without smudging on its delicate meniscus.
Children watch them playing in their heavenly playground;
Men use them to lug ships across oceans, through firths.

They seem so twinkle-still, but they never cease
Inventing new spaces and huge explosions
And migrating in mathematical tribes over
The steppes of space at their outrageous ease.

It's hard to think that the earth is one –
This poor sad bearer of wars and disasters
Rolls-Roycing round the sun with its load of gangsters,
Attended only by the loveless moon.

NORMAN MacCAIG (1910–96)

The Uncertainty of the Poet

I am a poet.
I am very fond of bananas.

I am bananas.
I am very fond of a poet.

I am a poet of bananas.
I am very fond.

A fond poet of 'I am, I am' –
Very bananas.

Fond of 'Am I bananas?
Am I?' – a very poet.

Bananas of a poet!
Am I fond? Am I very?

Poet bananas! I am.
I am fond of a 'very'.

I am of very fond bananas.
Am I a poet?

WENDY COPE (b. 1945)

'I saw a Peacock with a fiery tail'

I saw a Peacock with a fiery tail
I saw a blazing Comet drop down hail
I saw a Cloud with Ivy circled round
I saw a sturdy Oak creep on the ground
I saw a Pismire swallow up a Whale
I saw a raging Sea brim full of Ale
I saw a Venice Glass sixteen foot deep
I saw a Well full of men's tears that weep
I saw their Eyes all in a flame of fire
I saw a House as big as the Moon and higher
I saw the Sun even in the midst of night
I saw the Man that saw this wondrous sight.

ANON. (17th century)

from **Frost at Midnight**

The Frost performs its secret ministry,
Unhelped by any wind. The owlet's cry
Came loud – and hark, again! loud as before.
The inmates of my cottage, all at rest,
Have left me to that solitude, which suits
Abstruser musings: save that at my side
My cradled infant slumbers peacefully.
'Tis calm indeed! so calm, that it disturbs
And vexes meditation with its strange
And extreme silentness. Sea, hill, and wood,
This populous village! Sea, and hill, and wood,
With all the numberless goings-on of life,
Inaudible as dreams!

SAMUEL TAYLOR COLERIDGE (1772–1834)

Snow

The room was suddenly rich and the great bay-window was
Spawning snow and pink roses against it
Soundlessly collateral and incompatible:
World is suddener than we fancy it.

World is crazier and more of it than we think,
Incorrigibly plural. I peel and portion
A tangerine and spit the pips and feel
The drunkenness of things being various.

And the fire flames with a bubbling sound for world
Is more spiteful and gay than one supposes –
On the tongue on the eyes on the ears in the palms of one's
    hands –
There is more than glass between the snow and the huge
    roses.

LOUIS MacNEICE (1907–63)

On Himself

Abstracted by silence from the age of seven,
Deafened and penned by as black calamity
As twice to be born, I cannot without pity
Contemplate myself as an infant;

Or fail to speak of silence as a priestess
Calling to serve in the temple of a skull
Her innocent choice. It is barely possible
Not to be affected by such a distress.

DAVID WRIGHT (1920–94)

Sometimes

Sometimes things don't go, after all,
from bad to worse. Some years, muscadel
faces down frost; green thrives; the crops don't fail,
sometimes a man aims high, and all goes well.

A people sometimes will step back from war;
elect an honest man; decide they care
enough, that they can't leave some stranger poor.
Some men become what they were born for.

Sometimes our best efforts do not go
amiss; sometimes we do as we meant to.
The sun will sometimes melt a field of sorrow
that seemed hard frozen: may it happen for you.

SHEENAGH PUGH (b. 1950)

The Passionate Shepherd to his Love

Come live with me, and be my love,
And we will all the pleasures prove
That valleys, groves, hills and fields,
Woods, or steepy mountain yields.

And we will sit upon the rocks,
Seeing the shepherds feed their flocks
By shallow rivers, to whose falls
Melodious birds sing madrigals.

And I will make thee beds of roses,
And a thousand fragrant posies,
A cap of flowers, and a kirtle,
Embroidered all with leaves of myrtle.

A gown made of the finest wool
Which from our pretty lambs we pull,
Fair lined slippers for the cold,
With buckles of the purest gold.

A belt of straw and ivy buds,
With coral clasps and amber studs,
And if these pleasures may thee move,
Come live with me, and be my love.

The shepherds' swains shall dance and sing
For thy delight each May-morning;
If these delights thy mind may move,
Then live with me, and be my love.

CHRISTOPHER MARLOWE (1564–93)

Letter to André Billy. 9 April 1915

Gunner/Driver One (front-line)
Here I am and send you greetings
No no you're not seeing things
My Sector's number fifty-nine

I hear the whistle o_f
the   the bird
beautiful bird of pr^{e^y}

I see ^{far} away
the cathedral

O   D
H   E
M   A
Y A R
N D R E
B I L L Y

GUILLAUME APOLLINAIRE (1880–1918)
translated by OLIVER BERNARD

Child

Your clear eye is the one absolutely beautiful thing.
I want to fill it with colour and ducks,
The zoo of the new

Whose names you meditate –
April snowdrop, Indian pipe,
Little

Stalk without wrinkle,
Pool in which images
Should be grand and classical

Not this troublous
Wringing of hands, this dark
Ceiling without a star.

SYLVIA PLATH (1932–63)

A song for England

An' a so de rain a-fall
An' a so de snow a-rain

An' a so de fog a-fall
An' a so de sun a-fail

An' a so de seasons mix
An' a so de bag-o'-tricks

But a so me understan'
De misery o' de Englishman.

ANDREW SALKEY (1928–95)

Letters from Yorkshire

In February, digging his garden, planting potatoes,
he saw the first lapwings return and came
indoors to write to me, his knuckles singing

as they reddened in the warmth.
It's not romance, simply how things are.
You out there, in the cold, seeing the seasons

turning, me with my heartful of headlines
feeding words onto a blank screen.
Is your life more real because you dig and sow?

You wouldn't say so, breaking ice on a waterbutt,
clearing a path through snow. Still, it's you
who sends me word of that other world

pouring air and light into an envelope. So that
at night, watching the same news in different houses,
our souls tap out messages across the icy miles.

MAURA DOOLEY (b. 1957)

The Bonnie Broukit Bairn

Mars is braw in crammasy,
Venus in a green silk goun,
The auld mune shak's her gowden feathers,
Their starry talk's a wheen o' blethers,
Nane for thee a thochtie sparin',
Earth, thou bonnie broukit bairn!
– But greet, an' in your tears ye'll drown
The haill clanjamfrie!

HUGH MacDIARMID (CHRISTOPHER MURRAY GRIEVE)
(1892–1978)

braw: fine
crammasy: crimson
a wheen o' blethers: a pack of nonsense
broukit: neglected
greet: weep
the haill clanjamfrie: the whole caboodle

'Music, when soft voices die' Shelley's draft, extensively revised. Bodleian Library MS Shelley adds. e.8, p. 154 rev. By permission of The Bodleian Library, University of Oxford.

To Emilia V –

Music, when soft voices die,
Vibrates in the memory –
Odours, when sweet violets sicken,
Live within the sense they quicken.

Rose leaves, when the rose is dead,
Are heaped for the beloved's bed –
And so thy thoughts, when thou art gone,
Love itself shall slumber on . . .

PERCY BYSSHE SHELLEY (1792–1822)

Concerto for Double Bass

He is a drunk leaning companionably
Around a lamp post or doing up
With intermittent concentration
Another drunk's coat.

He is a polite but devoted Valentino,
Cheek to cheek, forgetting the next step.
He is feeling the pulse of the fat lady
Or cutting her in half.

But close your eyes and it is sunset
At the edge of the world. It is the language
Of dolphins, the growth of tree-roots,
The heart-beat slowing down.

JOHN FULLER (b. 1937)

Words, Wide Night

Somewhere on the other side of this wide night
and the distance between us, I am thinking of you.
The room is turning slowly away from the moon.

This is pleasurable. Or shall I cross that out and say
it is sad? In one of the tenses I singing
an impossible song of desire that you cannot hear.

La lala la. See? I close my eyes and imagine
the dark hills I would have to cross
to reach you. For I am in love with you and this

is what it is like or what it is like in words.

CAROL ANN DUFFY (b. 1955)

The Lobster Quadrille

'Will you walk a little faster?' said a whiting to a snail,
'There's a porpoise close behind us, and he's treading on my tail.
See how eagerly the lobsters and the turtles all advance!
They are waiting on the shingle – will you come and join the dance?
   Will you, won't you, will you, won't you,
     will you join the dance?
   Will you, won't you, will you, won't you,
     won't you join the dance?

'You can really have no notion how delightful it will be
When they take us up and throw us, with the lobsters, out to sea!'
But the snail replied 'Too far, too far!', and gave a look askance –
Said he thanked the whiting kindly, but he would not join the dance.
   Would not, could not, would not, could not,
     would not join the dance.
   Would not, could not, would not, could not,
     could not join the dance.

'What matters it how far we go?' his scaly friend replied.
'There is another shore, you know, upon the other side.
The further off from England the nearer is to France –
Then turn not pale, beloved snail, but come and join the dance.
   Will you, won't you, will you, won't you,
     will you join the dance?
   Will you, won't you, will you, won't you,
     won't you join the dance?'

LEWIS CARROLL (1832–98)

The Lobster Quadrille   Illustration by John Tenniel.

'I shall say what inordinate love is'

I shall say what inordinate love is:
The furiosity and wodness of mind,
An instinguible burning, faulting bliss,
A great hunger, insatiate to find,
A dulcet ill, an evil sweetness blind,
A right wonderful sugared sweet error,
Without labour rest, contrary to kind,
Or without quiet, to have huge labour.

ANON. (15th century)

wodness: frenzy

'I shall say what inordinate love is'   The only known source of this English version of a well-known Latin original. Thott 110, 4to., f. 163a. By permission of The Copenhagen Royal Library.

144

A red red Rose

O my Luve 's like a red, red rose,
   That's newly sprung in June;
O my Luve 's like the melodie
   That's sweetly play'd in tune.

As fair art thou, my bonnie lass,
   So deep in luve am I;
And I will love thee still, my Dear,
   Till a' the seas gang dry.

Till a' the seas gang dry, my Dear,
   And the rocks melt wi' the sun:
I will love thee still, my Dear,
   While the sands o' life shall run.

And fare thee weel, my only Luve!
   And fare thee weel, a while!
And I will come again, my Luve,
   Tho' it were ten thousand mile!

ROBERT BURNS (1759–96)

The Very Leaves of the Acacia-Tree are London

The very leaves of the acacia-tree are London;
London tap-water fills out the fuchsia buds in the back garden,
Blackbirds pull London worms out of the sour soil,
The woodlice, centipedes, eat London, the wasps even.
London air through stomata of myriad leaves
And million lungs of London breathes.
Chlorophyll and haemoglobin do what life can
To purify, to return this great explosion
To sanity of leaf and wing.
Gradual and gentle the growth of London Pride,
And sparrows are free of all the time in the world:
Less than a window-pane between.

KATHLEEN RAINE (1908–2003)

One Art

The art of losing isn't hard to master;
so many things seem filled with the intent
to be lost that their loss is no disaster.

Lose something every day. Accept the fluster
of lost door keys, the hour badly spent.
The art of losing isn't hard to master.

Then practice losing farther, losing faster:
places, and names, and where it was you meant
to travel. None of these will bring disaster.

I lost my mother's watch. And look! my last, or
next-to-last, of three loved houses went.
The art of losing isn't hard to master.

I lost two cities, lovely ones. And, vaster,
some realms I owned, two rivers, a continent.
I miss them, but it wasn't a disaster.

– Even losing you (the joking voice, a gesture
I love) I shan't have lied. It's evident
the art of losing's not too hard to master
though it may look like (*Write* it!) like disaster.

ELIZABETH BISHOP (1911–79)

To Someone Who Insisted I Look Up Someone

I rang them up while touring Timbuctoo,
Those bosom chums to whom you're known as *'Who?'*

X. J. KENNEDY (b. 1929)

Two Fragments

Love holds me captive again
and I tremble with bittersweet longing

As a gale on the mountainside bends the oak tree
I am rocked by my love

SAPPHO (fl. 600 BC)
translated by CICELY HERBERT

I Am

I am – yet what I am none cares or knows,
My friends forsake me like a memory lost;
I am the self-consumer of my woes,
They rise and vanish in oblivious host
Like shades in love and death's oblivion lost,
And yet I am – and live, with shadows tossed

Into the nothingness of scorn and noise,
Into the living sea of waking dreams,
Where there is neither sense of life nor joys,
But the vast shipwreck of my life's esteems;
And e'en the dearest, that I loved the best,
Are strange – nay, rather stranger than the rest.

I long for scenes where man has never trod,
A place where woman never smiled or wept,
There to abide with my creator, God,
And sleep as I in childhood sweetly slept,
Untroubling and untroubled where I lie;
The grass below – above the vaulted sky.

JOHN CLARE (1793–1864)

Dream Boogie

Good morning, daddy!
Ain't you heard
The boogie-woogie rumble
Of a dream deferred?

Listen closely:
You'll hear their feet
Beating out and beating out a –

You think
It's a happy beat?

Listen to it closely:
Ain't you heard
something underneath
like a —

What did I say?

Sure,
I'm happy!
Take it away!

Hey, pop!
Re-bop!
Mop!

Y-e-a-h!

LANGSTON HUGHES (1902–67)

The Unpredicted

The goddess Fortune be praised (on her toothed wheel
I have been mincemeat these several years)
Last night, for a whole night, the unpredictable
Lay in my arms, in a tender and unquiet rest –
(I perceived the irrelevance of my former tears) –
Lay, and at dawn departed. I rose and walked the streets
Where a whitsuntide wind blew fresh, and blackbirds
Incontestably sang, and the people were beautiful.

JOHN HEATH-STUBBS (b. 1918)

The Emigrant Irish

Like oil lamps we put them out the back,

of our houses, of our minds. We had lights
better than, newer than and then

a time came, this time and now
we need them. Their dread, makeshift example.

They would have thrived on our necessities.
What they survived we could not even live.
By their lights now it is time to
imagine how they stood there, what they stood with,
that their possessions may become our power.

Cardboard. Iron. Their hardships parcelled in them.
Patience. Fortitude. Long-suffering
in the bruise-coloured dusk of the New World.

And all the old songs. And nothing to lose.

EAVAN BOLAND (b. 1944)

from **The Garden**

What wondrous life in this I lead!
Ripe apples drop about my head;
The luscious clusters of the vine
Upon my mouth do crush their wine;
The nectarine, and curious peach,
Into my hands themselves do reach;
Stumbling on melons, as I pass,
Ensnared with flowers, I fall on grass.

Meanwhile the mind, from pleasure less,
Withdraws into its happiness:
The mind, that ocean where each kind
Does straight its own resemblance find;
Yet it creates, transcending these,
Far other worlds, and other seas;
Annihilating all that's made
To a green thought in a green shade.

ANDREW MARVELL (1621–78)

The Flaw in Paganism

Drink and dance and laugh and lie,
  Love, the reeling midnight through,
For tomorrow we shall die!
  (But, alas, we never do.)

DOROTHY PARKER (1893–1967)

The Algonquin Round Table   Dorothy Parker (lower left) surrounded by
Robert Benchley, Alfred Lunt and Lynn Fontanne, Frank Crowninshield,
Alexander Woollcott, Heywood Broun, Marc Connelly, Frank Case, Franklin
P. Adams, Edna Ferber, George Kaufman and Robert Sherwood. Illustration
by Al Hirschfeld.

Anthem for Doomed Youth

What passing-bells for these who die as cattle?
   – Only the monstrous anger of the guns.
   Only the stuttering rifles' rapid rattle
Can patter out their hasty orisons.
No mockeries now for them; no prayers nor bells;
   Nor any voice of mourning save the choirs, –
The shrill demented choirs of wailing shells;
   And bugles calling for them from sad shires.

What candles may be held to speed them all?
   Not in the hands of boys, but in their eyes
Shall shine the holy glimmers of goodbyes.
   The pallor of girls' brows shall be their pall;
Their flowers the tenderness of patient minds,
And each slow dusk a drawing-down of blinds.

WILFRED OWEN (1893–1918)

What passing-bells for these who die as cattle?
  — Only the monstrous anger of the guns.
  Only the stuttering rifles' rapid rattle
Can patter out their hasty orisons.
No {music for all them / mockeries} for them {nor / from} prayers nor or bells
  Nor any voice of mourning save the choirs,
The shrill demented disconsolate choirs of wailing shells;
  And bugles calling sad across the shires.
                    for them from sad

What candles may be held to speed them all?
  Not in the hands of boys, but in their eyes
Shall shine the holy glimmers of goodbyes.
And The pallor of girl's brows shall be their pall;
  Their flowers the tenderness of {silent / patient tender} minds,
And each slow dusk a drawing-down of blinds.

Anthem for Doomed Youth   The pencilled corrections are by Siegfried
Sassoon, Owen's friend and fellow poet. BL Add. MS 43720, f.17.
By permission of The British Library Board.

A Picture*

for Tiantian's fifth birthday

Morning arrives in a sleeveless dress
apples tumble all over the earth
my daughter is drawing a picture
how vast is a five-year-old sky
your name has two windows
one opens towards a sun with no clock-hands
the other opens towards your father
who has become a hedgehog in exile
taking with him a few unintelligible characters
and a bright red apple
he has left your painting
how vast is a five-year-old sky

BEI DAO (b. 1949)
translated by BONNIE S. McDOUGALL
and CHEN MAIPING

*Tiantian, the nickname given to the poet's daughter, is written with two characters which look like a pair of windows. The same character also forms a part of the character for the word 'picture'.

A Picture   The first two lines of the original poem. Calligraphy by
Yukki Yaura, © Yukki Yaura 1993 by permission of the artist.

Idyll

Not knowing even that we're on the way,
Until suddenly we're there. How shall we know?

There will be blackbirds, in a late March evening,
Blur of woodsmoke, whisky in grand glasses,

A poem of yours, waiting to be read; and one of mine;
A reflective bitch, a cat materialised

On a knee. All fears of present and future
Will be over, all guilts forgiven.

Maybe, heaven. Or maybe
We can get so far in this world. I'll believe we can.

U. A. FANTHORPE (b. 1929)

'Gray goose and gander'

Gray goose and gander,
   Waft your wings together,
And carry the good king's daughter
   Over the one strand river.

ANON. (date unknown)

Sonnet: On His Blindness

When I consider how my light is spent,
   Ere half my days, in this dark world and wide,
   And that one talent which is death to hide,
   Lodged with me useless, though my soul more bent
To serve therewith my maker, and present
   My true account, lest he returning chide,
   Doth God exact day-labour, light denied?
   I fondly ask; but Patience to prevent
That murmur, soon replies, God doth not need
   Either man's work or his own gifts, who best
   Bear his mild yoke, they serve him best, his state
Is kingly. Thousands at his bidding speed
   And post o'er land and ocean without rest:
   They also serve who only stand and wait.

JOHN MILTON (1608–74)

He wishes for the Cloths of Heaven

Had I the heavens' embroidered cloths,
Enwrought with golden and silver light,
The blue and the dim and the dark cloths
Of night and light and the half-light,
I would spread the cloths under your feet:
But I, being poor, have only my dreams;
I have spread my dreams under your feet;
Tread softly because you tread on my dreams.

W. B. YEATS (1865–1939)

Late Summer Fires

The paddocks shave black
with a foam of smoke that stays,
welling out of red-black wounds.

In the white of a drought
this happens. The hardcourt game.
Logs that fume are mostly cattle,

inverted, stubby. Tree stumps are kilns.
Walloped, wiped, hand-pumped,
even this day rolls over, slowly.

At dusk, a family drives sheep
out through the yellow
of the Aboriginal flag.

LES MURRAY (b. 1938)

Love in a Bathtub

Years later we'll remember the bathtub,
the position
           of the taps
the water, slippery
as if a bucketful
           of eels had joined us . . .
we'll be old, our children grown up
but we'll remember the water
                    sloshing out
the useless soap,
the mountain of wet towels.
'Remember the bathtub in Belfast?'
we'll prod each other –

SUJATA BHATT (b. 1956)

The Twa Corbies

As I was walking all alane,
I heard twa corbies making a mane;
The tane unto the tither say,
'Whar sall we gang and dine the day?'

'In behint yon auld fail dyke,
I wot there lies a new-slain knight;
And naebody kens that he lies there,
But his hawk, his hound, and lady fair.

'His hound is to the hunting gane,
His hawk to fetch the wild-fowl hame,
His lady's ta'en another mate,
Sae we may mak our dinner sweet.

'Ye'll sit on his white hause-bane,
And I'll pike out his bonnie blue een:
Wi' ae lock o' his gowden hair
We'll theek our nest when it grows bare.

'Mony a one for him makes mane,
But nane sall ken whar he is gane;
O'er his white banes, when they are bare,
The wind sall blaw for evermair.'

ANON. (before 1800)

corbie: raven   *mane:* moan   *hause-bane:* neck-bone

'The Great Frost'

O roving Muse, recall that wondrous year,
When winter reigned in bleak Britannia's air;
When hoary Thames, with frosted osiers crowned,
Was three long moons in icy fetters bound.
The waterman, forlorn along the shore,
Pensive reclines upon his useless oar,
Sees harnessed steeds desert the stony town,
And wander roads unstable, not their own;
Wheels o'er the hardened waters smoothly glide,
And rase with whitened tracks the slippery tide.
Here the fat cook piles high the blazing fire,
And scarce the spit can turn the steer entire.
Booths sudden hide the Thames, long streets appear,
And numerous games proclaim the crowded fair.

from TRIVIA,
OR THE ART OF WALKING THE STREETS OF LONDON

JOHN GAY (1685–1732)

If I Could Tell You

Time will say nothing but I told you so,
Time only knows the price we have to pay;
If I could tell you I would let you know.

If we should weep when clowns put on their show,
If we should stumble when musicians play,
Time will say nothing but I told you so.

There are no fortunes to be told, although,
Because I love you more than I can say,
If I could tell you I would let you know.

The winds must come from somewhere when they blow,
There must be reasons why the leaves decay;
Time will say nothing but I told you so.

Perhaps the roses really want to grow,
The vision seriously intends to stay;
If I could tell you I would let you know.

Suppose the lions all get up and go,
And all the brooks and soldiers run away;
Will Time say nothing but I told you so?
If I could tell you I would let you know.

W. H. AUDEN (1907–73)

Spacetime

When I grow up and you get small,
then –

(In Kaluza's theory the fifth dimension
is represented as a circle
associated with every point
in spacetime)

– then when I die, I'll never be alive again?
                Never.
Never never?
                Never never.
Yes, but never never never?
                No . . . not never never never,
                just never never.

So we made
a small family contribution
to the quantum problem of eleven-dimensional
   supergravity.

MIROSLAV HOLUB (1923–98)
translated by DAVID YOUNG *and* DANA HÁBOVÁ

Sun a-shine, rain a-fall

Sun a-shine an' rain a-fall,
The Devil an' him wife cyan 'gree at all,
The two o' them want one fish-head,
The Devil call him wife bonehead,
She hiss her teeth, call him cock-eye,
Greedy, worthless an' workshy,
While them busy callin' name,
The puss walk in, sey is a shame
To see a nice fish go to was'e,
Lef' with a big grin pon him face.

VALERIE BLOOM (b. 1956)

Sun a-shine, rain a-fall   Illustration by Michael Charlton.

Sonnet 18

Shall I compare thee to a summer's day?
Thou art more lovely and more temperate:
Rough winds do shake the darling buds of May,
And summer's lease hath all too short a date:
Sometime too hot the eye of heaven shines,
And often is his gold complexion dimmed;
And every fair from fair sometime declines,
By chance, or nature's changing course, untrimmed;
But thy eternal summer shall not fade,
Nor lose possession of that fair thou owest,
Nor shall death brag thou wander'st in his shade,
When in eternal lines to time thou growest;
   So long as men can breathe, or eyes can see,
   So long lives this, and this gives life to thee.

WILLIAM SHAKESPEARE (1564–1616)

A True and Faithful Inventory
of the Goods *belonging* to Dr. Swift, Vicar of *Lara Cor*;

upon lending his House to the Bishop of Meath,
until his own was built

An Oaken, broken, Elbow-Chair;
A Cawdle-Cup, without an Ear;
A batter'd, shatter'd Ash Bedstead;
A Box of Deal, without a Lid;
A Pair of Tongs, but out of Joint;
A Back-Sword Poker, without Point;
A Pot that's crack'd across, around,
With an old knotted Garter bound;
An iron lock, without a Key;
A Wig, with hanging, quite grown grey;
A Curtain worn to Half a Stripe;
A Pair of Bellows, without Pipe;
A Dish, which might good Meat afford once;
An *Ovid*, and an old *Concordance*;
A Bottle Bottom, Wooden Platter,
One is for Meal, and one for Water:
There likewise is a Copper Skillet,
Which runs as fast out as you fill it;
A Candlestick, Snuff dish, and Save-all,
And thus his Household Goods you have all.
These, to your Lordship, as a Friend,
Till you have built, I freely lend:
They'll save your Lordship for a Shift;
Why not, as well as Doctor *Swift*?

THOMAS SHERIDAN (1687–1738)

Where Go the Boats?

Dark brown is the river,
Golden is the sand.
It flows along for ever,
With trees on either hand.

Green leaves a-floating,
Castles of the foam,
Boats of mine a-boating –
Where will all come home?

On goes the river
And out past the mill,
Away down the valley,
Away down the hill.

Away down the river,
A hundred miles or more,
Other little children
Shall bring my boats ashore.

ROBERT LOUIS STEVENSON (1850–94)

Where Go the Boats?   Illustrations by A. H. Watson from
A Child's Garden of Verses, Collins (1946).

Thanks Forever

Look at those empty ships
floating north
between south-running ice
like big tulips
in the Narrows
under the Verrazano
toward the city harbor.
I'm parked here,
out of work all year.
No hurry now
and sleep badly.
But I'm self-employed.
My new job's
to wave them in.
Hello freighter,
hello tanker.
Welcome, welcome,
to New York.

MILTON KESSLER (1930–2000)

Swineherd

When all this is over, said the swineherd,
I mean to retire, where
Nobody will have heard about my special skills
And conversation is mainly about the weather.

I intend to learn how to make coffee, at least as well
As the Portuguese lay-sister in the kitchen
And polish the brass fenders every day.
I want to lie awake at night
Listening to cream crawling to the top of the jug
And the water lying soft in the cistern.

I want to see an orchard where the trees grow in straight lines
And the yellow fox finds shelter between the navy-blue trunks,
Where it gets dark early in summer
And the apple-blossom is allowed to wither on the bough.

EILÉAN NÍ CHUILLEANÁIN (b. 1942)

'The world is too much with us'

The world is too much with us; late and soon,
Getting and spending, we lay waste our powers:
Little we see in nature that is ours;
We have given our hearts away, a sordid boon!
This Sea that bares her bosom to the moon;
The Winds that will be howling at all hours
And are up-gathered now like sleeping flowers;
For this, for every thing, we are out of tune;
It moves us not. Great God! I'd rather be
A Pagan suckled in a creed outworn;
So might I, standing on this pleasant lea,
Have glimpses that would make me less forlorn;
Have sight of Proteus coming from the sea;
Or hear old Triton blow his wreathed horn.

WILLIAM WORDSWORTH (1770–1850)

The world is too much with us; late and soon
Getting and spending we lay waste our powers
Little we see in nature that is ours;
We have given our hearts away, a sordid boon.
This sea that bares her bosom to the moon
The winds that will be howling at all hours,
And are upgather'd now like sleeping flowers,
For this, for everything we are out of tune:
It moves us not. Great God! I'd rather be
A Pagan suckled in a creed outworn,
So might I, standing on this pleasant lea
Have glimpses that would make me less
Have sight of Proteus coming from the sea
Or hear old Triton blow his wreathed horn.

'The world is too much with us' From DC MS 44, a homemade notebook
of Wordsworth's then unpublished work, copied by his sister Dorothy and
his wife Mary, for Coleridge to take with him on a visit to Malta in 1804.
The hand on this poem is Dorothy Wordsworth's; the overlaid word 'hearts'
is written by William Wordsworth. DC MS 44 is one of the most important
sources of Wordsworth's early work. Reprinted by permission of The
Wordsworth Trust.

A Birthday

My heart is like a singing bird
   Whose nest is in a watered shoot;
My heart is like an apple-tree
   Whose boughs are bent with thick-set fruit;
My heart is like a rainbow shell
   That paddles in a halcyon sea;
My heart is gladder than all these
   Because my love is come to me.

Raise me a dais of silk and down;
   Hang it with vair and purple dyes;
Carve it in doves and pomegranates,
   And peacocks with a hundred eyes;
Work it in gold and silver grapes,
   In leaves and silver fleurs-de-lys;
Because the birthday of my life
   Is come, my love is come to me.

CHRISTINA ROSSETTI (1830–94)

Disillusionment of Ten O'Clock

The houses are haunted
By white night-gowns.
None are green,
Or purple with green rings,
Or green with yellow rings,
Or yellow with blue rings.
None of them are strange,
With socks of lace
And beaded ceintures.
People are not going
To dream of baboons and periwinkles.
Only, here and there, an old sailor,
Drunk and asleep in his boots,
Catches tigers
In red weather.

WALLACE STEVENS (1879–1955)

The Boundary Commission

You remember that village where the border ran
Down the middle of the street,
With the butcher and baker in different states?
Today he remarked how a shower of rain

Had stopped so cleanly across Golightly's lane
It might have been a wall of glass
That had toppled over. He stood there, for ages,
To wonder which side, if any, he should be on.

PAUL MULDOON (b. 1951)

Arrival 1946

The boat docked in at Liverpool.
From the train Tariq stared
at an unbroken line of washing
from the North West to Euston.

These are strange people, he thought –
an Empire, and all this washing,
the underwear, the Englishman's garden.
It was Monday, and very sharp.

MONIZA ALVI (b. 1954)

'Now winter nights enlarge'

Now winter nights enlarge
   The number of their hours
And clouds their storms discharge
   Upon the airy towers.
Let now the chimneys blaze,
   And cups o'erflow with wine:
Let well-tun'd words amaze
   With harmony divine.
Now yellow waxen lights
   Shall wait on honey Love,
While youthful Revels, Masks, and Courtly sights,
   Sleep's leaden spells remove.

This time doth well dispense
   With lovers' long discourse;
Much speech hath some defence,
   Though beauty no remorse.
All do not all things well;
   Some measures comely tread;
Some knotted Riddles tell;
   Some Poems smoothly read.
The Summer hath his joys,
   And Winter his delights;
Though Love and all his pleasures are but toys,
   They shorten tedious nights.

THOMAS CAMPION (1567–1620)

'Let my shadow disappear into yours'

Let my shadow disappear into yours.
Let me lose myself
under the tall trees,
that themselves lose their crowns in the twilight,
surrendering themselves to the sky and the night.

'Låt min skugga försvinna i din'

Låt min skugga försvinna i din.
Låt mig förlora mig själv
under de stora träden.
De som själva förlorar sin krona i skymningen,
överlämnar sig åt himmelen och natten.

PÄR LAGERKVIST (1891–1974)
translated by W. H. AUDEN *and* LEIF SJÖBERG

Do Not Go Gentle Into That Good Night

Do not go gentle into that good night,
Old age should burn and rave at close of day;
Rage, rage against the dying of the light.

Though wise men at their end know dark is right,
Because their words had forked no lightning they
Do not go gentle into that good night.

Good men, the last wave by, crying how bright
Their frail deeds might have danced in a green bay,
Rage, rage against the dying of the light.

Wild men who caught and sang the sun in flight,
And learn, too late, they grieved it on its way,
Do not go gentle into that good night.

Grave men, near death, who see with blinding sight
Blind eyes could blaze like meteors and be gay,
Rage, rage against the dying of the light.

And you, my father, there on the sad height,
Curse, bless, me now with your fierce tears, I pray.
Do not go gentle into that good night.
Rage, rage against the dying of the light.

DYLAN THOMAS (1914–53)

Look at all those monkeys

Look at all those monkeys
Jumping in their cage.
Why don't they all go out to work
And earn a decent wage?

> *How can you say such silly things,*
> *And you a son of mine?*
> *Imagine monkeys travelling on*
> *The Morden–Edgware line!*

But what about the Pekinese!
They have an allocation.
'Don't travel during Peke hour',
It says on every station.

> *My Gosh, you're right, my clever boy,*
> *I never thought of that!*
> And so they left the monkey house,
> While an elephant raised his hat.

SPIKE MILLIGAN (1918–2002)

Look at all those monkeys Drawing by the author, in *Silly Verse for Kids*,
© Spike Milligan, by permission of Spike Milligan Productions.

Mysteries

At night, I do not know who I am
when I dream, when I am sleeping.

Awakened, I hold my breath and listen:
a thumbnail scratches the other side of the wall.

At midday, I enter a sunlit room
to observe the lamplight on for no reason.

I should know by now that few octaves can be heard,
that a vision dies from being too long stared at;

that the whole of recorded history even
is but a little gossip in a great silence;

that a magnesium flash cannot illumine,
for one single moment, the invisible.

I do not complain. I start with the visible
and am startled by the visible.

DANNIE ABSE (b. 1923)

Rooms

Though I love this travelling life and yearn
like ships docked, I long
for rooms to open with my bare hands,
and there discover the wonderful, say
a ship's prow rearing, and a ladder
of rope thrown down.
Though young, I'm weary:
I'm all rooms at present, all doors
fastened against me;
but once admitted start craving
and swell for a fine, listing ocean-going prow
no man in creation can build me.

KATHLEEN JAMIE (b. 1962)

The Good Morrow

I wonder, by my troth, what thou and I
Did, till we loved; were we not weaned till then,
But sucked on country pleasures, childishly?
Or snorted we in the Seven Sleepers' den?
'Twas so; but this, all pleasures fancies be.
If ever any beauty I did see,
Which I desired, and got, 'twas but a dream of thee.

And now good morrow to our waking souls,
Which watch not one another out of fear;
For love, all love of other sights controls,
And makes one little room, an everywhere.
Let sea-discoverers to new worlds have gone,
Let maps to others, worlds on worlds have shown,
Let us possess our world; each hath one, and is one.

My face in thine eye, thine in mine appears,
And true plain hearts do in the faces rest;
Where can we find two better hemispheres,
Without sharp North, without declining West?
Whatever dies, was not mixed equally;
If our two loves be one; or thou and I
Love so alike that none do slacken, none can die.

JOHN DONNE (1572–1631)

Adlestrop

Yes. I remember Adlestrop –
The name, because one afternoon
Of heat the express-train drew up there
Unwontedly. It was late June.

The steam hissed. Someone cleared his throat.
No one left and no one came
On the bare platform. What I saw
Was Adlestrop – only the name

And willows, willow-herb, and grass,
And meadowsweet, and haycocks dry,
No whit less still and lonely fair
Than the high cloudlets in the sky.

And for that minute a blackbird sang
Close by, and round him, mistier,
Farther and farther, all the birds
Of Oxfordshire and Gloucestershire.

EDWARD THOMAS (1878–1917)

from **Requiem**

The hour of remembrance has drawn close again.
I see you, hear you, feel you:

the one they could hardly get to the window,
the one who no longer walks on this earth,

the one who shook her beautiful head,
and said: 'Coming here is like coming home.'

I would like to name them all but they took away
the list and there's no way of finding them.

For them I have woven a wide shroud
from the humble words I heard among them.

I remember them always, everywhere,
I will never forget them, whatever comes.

ANNA AKHMATOVA (1889–1966)
translated by RICHARD McKANE

The Exiles

translated from the author's own Gaelic

The many ships that left our country
with white wings for Canada.
They are like handkerchiefs in our memories
and the brine like tears
and in their masts sailors singing
like birds on branches.
That sea of May running in such blue,
a moon at night, a sun at daytime,
and the moon like a yellow fruit,
like a plate on a wall
to which they raise their hands
like a silver magnet
with piercing rays
streaming into the heart.

IAIN CRICHTON SMITH (1928–98)

Moonwise
(for my children, all)

sometimes
you know
the moon
is not such a perfect
circle

and the master Painter
makes a passing
brush touch
with a cloud

don't worry
we've passed
the dark side

all you children
rest easy now

we are born

moonwise

JEAN 'BINTA' BREEZE (b. 1956)

'My true love hath my heart and I have his'

My true love hath my heart and I have his,
By just exchange one for the other given.
I hold his dear, and mine he cannot miss,
There never was a better bargain driven.
　　My true love hath my heart and I have his.

His heart in me keeps me and him in one,
My heart in him his thoughts and senses guides:
He loves my heart, for once it was his own,
I cherish his because in me it bides.
　　My true love hath my heart, and I have his.

SIR PHILIP SIDNEY (1554–86)

Acquainted with the Night

I have been one acquainted with the night.
I have walked out in rain – and back in rain.
I have outwalked the furthest city light.

I have looked down the saddest city lane.
I have passed by the watchman on his beat
And dropped my eyes, unwilling to explain.

I have stood still and stopped the sound of feet
When far away an interrupted cry
Came over houses from another street,

But not to call me back or say good-by;
And further still at an unearthly height
One luminary clock against the sky

Proclaimed the time was neither wrong nor right.
I have been one acquainted with the night.

ROBERT FROST (1874–1963)

from **Summoned by Bells**

Great was my joy with London at my feet –
All London mine, five shillings in my hand
And not expected back till after tea!
Great was our joy, Ronald Hughes Wright's and mine,
To travel by the Underground all day
Between the rush hours, so that very soon
There was no station, north to Finsbury Park,
To Barking eastwards, Clapham Common south,
No temporary platform in the west
Among the Actons and the Ealings, where
We had not once alighted. Metroland
Beckoned us out to lanes in beechy Bucks –
Goldschmidt and Howland (in a wooden hut
Beside the station): 'Most attractive sites
Ripe for development'; Charrington's for coal;
And not far off the neo-Tudor shops.

JOHN BETJEMAN (1906–84)

Summoned by Bells 'The Underground' by Hugh Casson, from *The
Illustrated Summoned by Bells*, with paintings and sketches by Hugh Casson
(John Murray 1989). By permission of the artist. © Hugh Casson 1989.

A Glass of Water

Here is a glass of water from my well.
It tastes of rock and root and earth and rain;
It is the best I have, my only spell,
And it is cold, and better than champagne.
Perhaps someone will pass this house one day
To drink, and be restored, and go his way,
Someone in dark confusion as I was
When I drank down cold water in a glass,
Drank a transparent health to keep me sane,
After the bitter mood had gone again.

MAY SARTON (1912–95)

Wind

This is the wind, the wind in a field of corn.
Great crowds are fleeing from a major disaster
Down the long valleys, the green swaying wadis,
Down through the beautiful catastrophe of wind.

Families, tribes, nations and their livestock
Have heard something, seen something. An expectation
Or a gigantic misunderstanding has swept over the hilltop
Bending the ear of the hedgerow with stories of fire and sword.

I saw a thousand years pass in two seconds.
Land was lost, languages rose and divided.
This lord went east and found safety.
His brother sought Africa and a dish of aloes.

Centuries, minutes later, one might ask
How the hilt of a sword wandered so far from the smithy.
And somewhere they will sing: 'Like chaff we were borne
In the wind.' This is the wind in a field of corn.

JAMES FENTON (b. 1949)

To My Dear and Loving Husband

If ever two were one, then surely we.
If ever man were loved by wife, then thee;
If ever wife was happy in a man,
Compare with me ye women if you can.
I prize thy love more than whole mines of gold,
Or all the riches that the East doth hold.
My love is such that rivers cannot quench,
Nor ought but love from thee give recompence.
Thy love is such I can no way repay,
The heavens reward thee manifold I pray.
Then while we live, in love let's so persever,
That when we live no more, we may live ever.

ANNE BRADSTREET (1612–72)

Chorus from a Play
(written in the year 1700)

All, all, of a piece throughout;
Thy chase had a beast in view;
Thy wars brought nothing about;
Thy lovers were all untrue.
'Tis well an old age is out,
And time to begin a new.

JOHN DRYDEN (1631–1700)

Inversnaid

This dárksome búrn, hórseback brówn,
His rollrock highroad roaring down,
In coop and in comb the fleece of his foam
Flutes and low to the lake falls home.

A windpuff-bónnet of fáwn-fróth
Turns and twindles over the broth
Of a pool so pitchblack, féll-frówning,
It rounds and rounds Despair to drowning.

Degged with dew, dappled with dew
Are the groins of the braes that the brook treads through,
Wiry heathpacks, flitches of fern,
And the beadbonny ash that sits over the burn.

What would the world be, once bereft
Of wet and of wildness? Let them be left,
O let them be left, wildness and wet;
Long live the weeds and the wilderness yet.

GERARD MANLEY HOPKINS (1844–89)

Saturday Morning

Everyone who made love the night before
was walking around with flashing red lights
on top of their heads – a white-haired old gentleman,
a red-faced schoolboy, a pregnant woman
who smiled at me from across the street
and gave a little secret shrug,
as if the flashing red light on her head
was a small price to pay for what she knew.

HUGO WILLIAMS (b. 1942)

The Undertaking

The darkness lifts, imagine, in your lifetime.
There you are – cased in clean bark you drift
through weaving rushes, fields flooded with cotton.
You are free. The river films with lilies,
shrubs appear, shoots thicken into palm. And now
all fear gives way: the light
looks after you, you feel the waves' goodwill
as arms widen over the water; Love,

the key is turned. Extend yourself –
it is the Nile, the sun is shining,
everywhere you turn is luck.

LOUISE GLÜCK (b. 1943)

His Return to London

From the dull confines of the drooping West,
To see the day spring from the pregnant East,
Ravished in spirit, I come, nay more, I fly
To thee, blest place of my nativity!
Thus, thus with hallowed foot I touch the ground,
With thousand blessings by thy fortune crowned.
O fruitful Genius! that bestowest here
An everlasting plenty, year by year.
O place! O people! Manners! framed to please
All nations, customs, kindreds, languages!
I am a free-born Roman; suffer then,
That I amongst you live a citizen.
London my home is: though by hard fate sent
Into a long and irksome banishment;
Yet since called back; henceforward let me be,
O native country, repossessed by thee!
For, rather than I'll to the West return,
I'll beg of thee first here to have mine urn.
Weak I am grown, and must in short time fall;
Give thou my sacred relics burial.

ROBERT HERRICK (1591–1674)

'I taste a liquor never brewed'

I taste a liquor never brewed –
From Tankards scooped in Pearl –
Not all the Vats upon the Rhine
Yield such an Alcohol!

Inebriate of Air – am I –
And Debauchee of Dew –
Reeling – thro endless summer days –
From inns of Molten Blue –

When "Landlords" turn the drunken Bee
Out of the Foxglove's door –
When Butterflies – renounce their "drams" –
I shall but drink the more!

Till Seraphs swing their snowy Hats –
And Saints – to windows run –
To see the little Tippler
Leaning against the – Sun –

EMILY DICKINSON (1830–86)

The Poet

Therefore he no more troubled the pool of silence.
But put on mask and cloak,
Strung a guitar
And moved among the folk.
Dancing they cried,
'Ah, how our sober islands
Are gay again, since this blind lyrical tramp
Invaded the Fair!'

Under the last dead lamp
When all the dancers and masks had gone inside
His cold stare
Returned to its true task, interrogation of silence.

GEORGE MACKAY BROWN (1921–96)

Greenwich Park

Spring's come, a little late, in the park:
a tree-rat smokes flat S's over the lawn.
A mallard has somehow forgotten something
it can't quite remember. Daffodils yawn,
prick their ears, push their muzzles out
for a kiss. Pansies spoof pensive
Priapus faces: Socrates or Verlaine.
A cock-pigeon is sexually harassing
a hen: pecking and poking and padding
behind her impertinently, bowing and mowing.
But when he's suddenly absent-minded –
can't keep even sex in his head –
she trembles, stops her gadding, doubts
and grazes his way. He remembers and pouts.

HERBERT LOMAS (b. 1924)

Apology

Humming your Nocturne on the Circle Line,
unlike the piano, running out of breath

I've been writing you out of my life
my loves (one out, one in).

I've pushed you out of the way to see
what the gaps in my life might look like,

how large they are,
how quickly I could write them in;

and not (at least till I've lost you both)
rewriting you only means

that the spaces I'm not writing in are where
I live.

MIMI KHALVATI (b. 1944)

'Under the greenwood tree'

Under the greenwood tree
Who loves to lie with me,
And turn his merry note
Unto the sweet bird's throat,
Come hither, come hither, come hither:
    Here shall he see
    No enemy
But winter and rough weather.

Who doth ambition shun
And loves to live i' th' sun,
Seeking the food he eats,
And pleased with what he gets,
Come hither, come hither, come hither:
    Here shall he see
    No enemy
But winter and rough weather.

from AS YOU LIKE IT

WILLIAM SHAKESPEARE (1564–1616)

from Poetry

And it was at that age . . . Poetry arrived
in search of me. I don't know, I don't know where
it came from, from winter or a river.
I don't know how or when,
no, they were not voices, they were not
words, nor silence,
but from a street I was summoned,
from the branches of night,
abruptly from the others,
among violent fires
or returning alone,
there I was without a face
and it touched me.

from La poesía

Y fue a esa edad . . . Llegó la poesía
a buscarme. No sé, no sé de dónde
salió, de invierno o río.
No sé cómo ni cuándo,
no, no eran voces, no eran
palabras, ni silencio,
pero desde una calle me llamaba,
desde las ramas de la noche,
de pronto entre los otros,
entre fuegos violentos
o regresando solo,
allí estaba sin rostro
y me tocaba.

PABLO NERUDA (1904–73)
translated by ALASTAIR REID

Memory of my Father

Every old man I see
Reminds me of my father
When he had fallen in love with death
One time when sheaves were gathered.

That man I saw in Gardner Street
Stumble on the kerb was one,
He stared at me half-eyed,
I might have been his son.

And I remember the musician
Faltering over his fiddle
In Bayswater, London,
He too set me the riddle.

Every old man I see
In October-coloured weather
Seems to say to me:
'I was once your father.'

PATRICK KAVANAGH (1906–67)

Secret Lives

Sometimes your dressing gown unhooks
and slides out under the garden door,
with three aces up his sleeve.

He flies in the face of next door's dog,
and backflips down the middle of the street,
opening himself and humming.

Something in pink nylon flutters at him
from a bedroom window. He twirls his cord
to beckon her outside.

They're heading for a club they know
where the dress code is relaxed midweek,
and the music is strictly soul.

SIÂN HUGHES

Potosí

The moon falls
like a metaphysician
on the silver city

so distressed a metal –
even the horses shod with silver
in the freezing streets

wagons, blue with graffiti
under the spoil-tips,
and at first light

mountain foxes,
red as cinnabar,
moving against the flow

between the silver-bearing lodes,
the upland snow.

PAULINE STAINER

The Lesson (an anti-pastoral)

The small schoolgirl
   on her way down
      grey Portugal Lane
      late for class
who brushes a careless
   hand against
      the one green
         nettle that had to sprout
      from yards of concrete
can't believe
   there's no dock leaf
            to cancel
            it out.

TRACY RYAN

213

'My lefe ys faren in a lond'

My love is faren in a land;
Alas why is she so?
And I am so sore bound
I may not come her to.
She hath my heart in hold
Wherever she ride or go,
With true love a thousandfold.

ANON. (15th century)

'My lefe ys faren in a lond'   Trinity MS R.3.19, f. 154a, reproduced by permission of the Master and Fellows, Trinity College, Cambridge.

from **Ecclesiastes**

What profit hath a man of all his labour which he taketh under
   the sun?

One generation passeth away, and another generation cometh:
   but the earth abideth for ever.

The sun also ariseth, and the sun goeth down, and hasteth to
   his place where he arose.

The wind goeth toward the south, and turneth about unto the
   north; it whirleth about continually, and the wind returneth
   again according to his circuits.

All the rivers run into the sea; yet the sea is not full; unto the
   place from whence the rivers come, thither they return
   again.

THE KING JAMES BIBLE (1611)

Nightsong: City

Sleep well, my love, sleep well:
the harbour lights glaze over restless docks,
police cars cockroach through the tunnel streets;

from the shanties creaking iron-sheets
violence like a bug-infested rag is tossed
and fear is immanent as sound in the wind-swung bell;

the long day's anger pants from sand and rocks;
but for this breathing night at least,
my land, my love, sleep well.

DENNIS BRUTUS (b. 1924)

Shopper

I am spending my way out
of a recession. The road chokes
on delivery vans.

I used to be Just Looking Round,
I used to be How Much, and
Have You Got it in Beige.

Now I devour whole stores –
high speed spin; giant size; chunky gold;
de luxe springing. Things.

I drag them round me into a stockade.
It is dark inside; but my credit cards
are incandescent.

CONNIE BENSLEY (b. 1929)

The Rescue

In drifts of sleep I came upon you
Buried to your waist in snow.
You reached your arms out: I came to
Like water in a dream of thaw.

SEAMUS HEANEY (b. 1939)

Rondel

The weather's cast its cloak of grey
Woven of wind and cold and rain,
And wears embroidered clothes again
Of clear sunshine, in fair array.
   No beast, no bird, but in its way
Cries out or sings in wood and plain:
The weather's cast its cloak of grey
Woven of wind and cold and rain.
   River and spring and brook this day
Wear handsome liveries that feign
More silver stars than Charles's Wain,
Mingled with drops of golden spray.
The weather's cast its cloak of grey.

Rondel

Le temps a laissié son manteau
De vent, de froidure et de pluye,
Et s'est vestu de brouderie,
De soleil luyant, cler et beau.
   Il n'y a beste, ne oyseau,
Qu'en son jargon ne chant ou crie:
Le temps a laissié son manteau
De vent, de froidure et de pluye.
   Rivière, fontaine et ruisseau
Portent, en livrée jolie,
Gouttes d'argent d'orfaverie,
Chascun s'abille de nouveau.
Le temps a laissié son manteau.

CHARLES D'ORLÉANS (1394–1465)
translated by OLIVER BERNARD

from **An Essay on Man**

Know then thyself, presume not God to scan;
The proper study of Mankind is Man.
Plac'd on this isthmus of a middle state,
A being darkly wise, and rudely great:
With too much knowledge for the Sceptic side,
With too much weakness for the Stoic's pride,
He hangs between; in doubt to act, or rest,
In doubt to deem himself a God, or Beast;
In doubt his Mind or Body to prefer,
Born but to die, and reas'ning but to err;
Alike in ignorance, his reason such,
Whether he thinks too little, or too much:
Chaos of Thought and Passion, all confus'd;
Still by himself abus'd, or disabus'd;
Created half to rise, and half to fall;
Great lord of all things, yet a prey to all;
Sole judge of Truth, in endless Error hurl'd:
The glory, jest, and riddle of the world!

EPISTLE II, 1–18

ALEXANDER POPE (1688–1744)

Le Faune.

—

Un vieux Faune de terre cuite
Rit au centre des boulingrins,
Présageant sans doute une suite
Mauvaise à ces instants sereins

Qui m'ont conduit et t'ont conduite,
— Mélancoliques pèlerins, —
Jusqu'à cette heure dont la fuite
Tournoie au son des tambourins

Le Faune Autograph manuscript from the poet's fair copy of *Fêtes galantes* in the Stefan Zweig Collection, The British Library. BL Zweig MS. 195. By permission of The British Library Board.

The Faun

In the middle of the sporting green
Taunts an old terra-cotta faun;
Predicting, no doubt, a sour outcome

To those idylls, so serene,
Which lured us, melancholy pilgrims,
To this meeting, already fleeting,

To the skirl of tambourines.

Le Faune

Un vieux faune de terre cuite
Rit au centre des boulingrins,
Présageant sans doute une suite
Mauvaise à ces instants sereins

Qui m'ont conduit et t'ont conduite,
– Mélancoliques pèlerins –
Jusqu'à cette heure dont la fuite
Tournoie au son des tambourins.

PAUL VERLAINE (1844–96)
translated by JOHN MONTAGUE

Cargoes

Quinquireme of Nineveh from distant Ophir
Rowing home to haven in sunny Palestine,
With a cargo of ivory,
And apes and peacocks,
Sandalwood, cedarwood, and sweet white wine.

Stately Spanish galleon coming from the Isthmus,
Dipping through the Tropics by the palm-green shores,
With a cargo of diamonds,
Emeralds, amethysts,
Topazes, and cinnamon, and gold moidores.

Dirty British coaster with a salt-caked smoke stack
Butting through the Channel in the mad March days,
With a cargo of Tyne coal,
Road-rails, pig-lead,
Firewood, iron-ware, and cheap tin trays.

JOHN MASEFIELD (1878–1967)

Waiting for Rain in Devon

Rain here on a tableau of cows
might seem a return to everyday –
why, you can almost poach
the trout with your hands,
their element has so thickened!
Something has emerged from dreams
to show us where we are going,
a journey to a desolate star.
Come back, perennial rain,
stand your soft sculptures in our gardens
for the barefoot frogs to leap.

PETER PORTER (b. 1929)

Wedding

From time to time our love is like a sail
and when the sail begins to alternate
from tack to tack, it's like a swallowtail
and when the swallow flies it's like a coat;
and if the coat is yours, it has a tear
like a wide mouth and when the mouth begins
to draw the wind, it's like a trumpeter
and when the trumpet blows, it blows like millions . . .
and this, my love, when millions come and go
beyond the need of us, is like a trick;
and when the trick begins, it's like a toe
tip-toeing on a rope, which is like luck;
and when the luck begins, it's like a wedding,
which is like love, which is like everything.

ALICE OSWALD (b. 1966)

from **Mutabilitie**

Then came the *Autumne* all in yellow clad,
  As though he joyed in his plentious store,
  Laden with fruits that made him laugh, full glad
  That he had banisht hunger, which to-fore
  Had by the belly oft him pinched sore.
  Upon his head a wreath that was enrold
  With eares of corne of every sort he bore:
  And in his hand a sickle he did holde,
To reape the ripened fruits the which the earth had yold.

THE FAERIE QUEENE, Canto VII, stanza 30

EDMUND SPENSER (1552–99)

Fernando Pessoa Sketch by Júlio Pomar, in *A Centenary Pessoa*, edited by Eugénio Lisboa with L. C. Taylor (Carcanet 1995). One in a series of preliminary drawings for a mural in the 'Alto dos Moinhos' station of the Lisbon Underground. By permission of the artist and the Calouste Gulbenkian Foundation.

Harvestwoman

But no, she's abstract, is a bird
Of sound in the air of air soaring,
And her soul sings unencumbered
Because the song's what makes her sing.

Ceifeira

Mas não, é abstrata, é uma ave
De som volteando no ar do ar,
E a alma canta sem entrave
Pois que o canto é que faz cantar.

FERNANDO PESSOA (1888–1935)
translated by JONATHAN GRIFFIN

Expectans Expectavi

The candid freezing season again:
Candle and cracker, needles of fir and frost;
Carols that through the night air pass, piercing
The glassy husk of heart and heaven;
Children's faces white in the pane, bright in the tree-light.

And the waiting season again,
That begs a crust and suffers joy vicariously:
In bodily starvation now, in the spirit's exile always.
O might the hilarious reign of love begin, let in
Like carols from the cold
The lost who crowd the pane, numb outcasts into welcome.

ANNE RIDLER (1912–2001)

Mama Dot

Born on a sunday
in the kingdom of Ashante

Sold on monday
into slavery

Ran away on tuesday
cause she born free

Lost a foot on wednesday
when they catch she

Worked all thursday
till her head grey

Dropped on friday
where they burned she

Freed on saturday
in a new century

FRED D'AGUIAR (b. 1960)

Voyage to the Bottom of the Sea

The trick (he tells me) is to sleep till twelve
    then watch the television.
In the corner of his murky bedroom
    there is always a swirl of colour:

T-shirts; smoke threading from an ashtray
    to the light; shoes; anemones thriving
on the wreck of the Torrey Canyon;
    our Chancellor raising the Budget box.

STEPHEN KNIGHT (b. 1960)

Sic Vita

Like to the falling of a star;
Or as the flights of eagles are;
Or like the fresh spring's gaudy hue;
Or silver drops of morning dew;
Or like a wind that chafes the flood;
Or bubbles which on water stood;
Even such is man, whose borrowed light
Is straight called in, and paid to night.

The wind blows out; the bubble dies;
The spring entombed in autumn lies;
The dew dries up; the star is shot;
The flight is past; and man forgot.

HENRY KING (1592–1669)

from **Dover Beach**

The sea is calm tonight.
The tide is full, the moon lies fair
Upon the straits; – on the French coast the light
Gleams and is gone; the cliffs of England stand,
Glimmering and vast, out in the tranquil bay.
Come to the window, sweet is the night air!
Only, from the long line of spray
Where the sea meets the moon-blanched land,
Listen! you hear the grating roar
Of pebbles which the waves draw back, and fling,
At their return, up the high strand,
Begin, and cease, and then again begin,
With tremulous cadence slow, and bring
The eternal note of sadness in.

. . . Ah, love, let us be true
To one another! for the world, which seems
To lie before us like a land of dreams,
So various, so beautiful, so new,
Hath really neither joy, nor love, nor light,
Nor certitude, nor peace, nor help for pain;
And we are here as on a darkling plain
Swept with confused alarms of struggle and flight,
Where ignorant armies clash by night.

MATTHEW ARNOLD (1822–88)

The Reassurance

About ten days or so
After we saw you dead
You came back in a dream.
I'm all right now you said.

And it *was* you, although
You were fleshed out again:
You hugged us all round then,
And gave your welcoming beam.

How like you to be kind,
Seeking to reassure.
And, yes, how like my mind
To make itself secure.

THOM GUNN (1929–2004)

Don't Call Alligator Long-Mouth
till You Cross River

Call alligator long-mouth
call alligator saw-mouth
call alligator pushy-mouth
call alligator scissors-mouth
call alligator raggedy-mouth
call alligator bumpy-bum
call alligator all dem rude word
but better wait
                till you cross river.

JOHN AGARD (b. 1949)

The Language Issue

I place my hope on the water
in this little boat
of the language, the way a body might put
an infant

in a basket of intertwined
iris leaves,
its underside proofed
with bitumen and pitch,

then set the whole thing down amidst
the sedge
and bulrushes by the edge
of a river

only to have it borne hither and thither,
not knowing where it might end up;
in the lap, perhaps,
of some Pharaoh's daughter.

NUALA NÍ DHOMHNAILL (b. 1952)
translated from the Irish by PAUL MULDOON

Longings

Like the beautiful bodies of those who died before growing old,
sadly shut away in a sumptuous mausoleum,
roses by the head, jasmine at the feet –
so appear the longings that have passed
without being satisfied, not one of them granted
a single night of pleasure, or one of its radiant mornings.

Επιθυμίες

Σὰν σώματα ὡραῖα νεκρῶν ποὺ δὲν ἐγέρασαν
καὶ τἄκλεισαν, μὲ δάκρυα, σὲ μαυσωλεῖο λαμπρό,
μὲ ρόδα στὸ κεφάλι καὶ στὰ πόδια γιασεμιὰ –
ἔτσ' ἡ ἐπιθυμίες μοιάζουν ποὺ ἐπέρασαν
χωρὶς νὰ ἐκπληρωθοῦν· χωρὶς ν' ἀξιωθεῖ καμιὰ
τῆς ἡδονῆς μιὰ νύχτα, ἤ ἕνα πρωΐ της φεγγερό.

C. P. CAVAFY (1863–1933)
translated by EDMUND KEELEY *and* PHILIP SHERRARD

Hope

I want to let go –
so I don't give a damn about fine writing,
I'm rolling my sleeves up.
The dough's rising . . .
Oh what a shame
I can't bake cathedrals . . .
that sublimity of style
I've always yearned for . . .
Child of our time –
haven't you found the right shell for your soul?
Before I die I *shall*
bake a cathedral.

Förhoppning

Jag vill vara ogenerad –
därför struntar jag i ädla stilar,
ärmarna kavlar jag upp.
Diktens deg jäser . . .
O en sorg –
att ej kunna baka katedraler . . .
Formernas höghet –
trägna längtans mål.
Nutidens barn –
har din ande ej sitt rätta skal?
Innan jag dör
bakar jag en katedral.

EDITH SÖDERGRAN (1892–1923)
translated by HERBERT LOMAS

'Lunar Pierrot'   Drawing by Federico García Lorca, © Herederos de
Federico García Lorca (see Acknowledgements, p.316).

Peaceful Waters: Variation

peaceful waters of the air
under an echo's branches

peaceful waters of a pool
under a bough laden with stars

peaceful waters of your mouth
under a forest of kisses

Remansos: Variación

El remanso del aire
bajo la rama del eco.

El remanso del agua
bajo fronda de luceros.

El remanso de tu boca
bajo espesura de besos.

FEDERICO GARCÍA LORCA (1898–1936)
translated by ADRIAN MITCHELL

'Fresh sighs for sale'

Fresh sighs for sale!
Prime doubts a penny!
Scowls going at a loss!
When I'm sold out I'll go
far from me and these among
be born again:
a mango warm from the bough,
a more than feline kiss,
a few objects without name.
Fresh hopes for sale!
Prime sooth a penny!
Smiles going at a loss!
Bargains, bargains, in and out of reason!

'Achetez mes soupirs'

Achetez mes soupirs.
Prenez mes doutes.
Je vous donne un cornet de grimaces?
Quand j'aurai tout vendu,
j'irai renaître loin de moi,
entre une mangue fraîche,
un baiser très félin,
quelques objets sans nom.
Achetez mes espoirs.
Prenez mes certitudes.
Je vous donne un cornet de sourires?
Je suis le marchand des quatre raisons.

ALAIN BOSQUET (1919–98)
translated by SAMUEL BECKETT

25 February 1944

I wish I could believe in something beyond,
Beyond the death that has undone you.
I wish I could tell of the strength
With which we longed then,
Already drowned,
To walk together once again
Free under the sun.

January 9, 1946

25 febbraio 1944

Vorrei credere qualcosa oltre,
Oltre che morte ti ha disfatta.
Vorrei poter dire la forza
Con cui desiderammo allora,
Noi già sommersi,
Di potere ancora una volta insieme
Camminare liberi sotto il sole.

9 gennaio 1946

PRIMO LEVI (1919–87)
translated by ELEONORA CHIAVETTA

25th April 1974

This is the dawn I was waiting for
The first day whole and pure
When we emerged from night and silence
Alive into the substance of time

25 de Abril

Esta é a madrugada que eu esperava
O dia inicial inteiro e limpo
Onde emergimos da noite e do silêncio
E livres habitamos a substância do tempo

SOPHIA DE MELLO BREYNER (b. 1919)
translated by RUTH FAINLIGHT

25 April 1974: The date of a peaceful left-wing army coup (the 'Carnation Revolution'), ending forty-eight years of dictatorship in Portugal.

A Collector

The things I found
But they'll scatter them again
to the four winds
as soon as I am dead

Old gadgets
fossilised plants and shells
books broken dolls
coloured postcards

And all the words
I have found
my incomplete
my unsatisfied words

Ein Sammler

Meine Funde
Aber sie werden sie wieder
zerstreuen in alle vier Winde
wenn ich erst tot bin

Alte Geräte
versteinerte Pflanzen und Tiere
bunte Postkarten Bücher
zerbrochene Puppen

Auch alle Worte
die ich gefunden habe
meine unvollständigen
meine ungesättigten Worte

ERICH FRIED (1921–88)
translated by STUART HOOD

'Somewhere in the house'

Somewhere in the house
a door slams shut
and a small giraffe
of bright orange plastic
totters briefly.
A present from a six-year-old
boy who, commuting
between bewildered parents,
bears his fate with
incomprehensible joy.

'Ergens in huis'

Ergens in huis
slaat hard een deur dicht
en even wankelt
de kleine giraffe
van vrolijk oranje plastic.
Geschenk van een 6-jarig
jongetje dat pendelend
tussen ontredderde ouders
zijn lot onbegrijpelijk
blijmoedig draagt.

HANNY MICHAELIS (b. 1922)
translated by MARJOLIJN DE JAGER

Distances

Swifts turn in the heights of the air;
higher still turn the invisible stars.
When day withdraws to the ends of the earth
their fires shine on a dark expanse of sand.

We live in a world of motion and distance.
The heart flies from tree to bird,
from bird to distant star,
from star to love; and love grows
in the quiet house, turning and working,
servant of thought, a lamp held in one hand.

Les distances

Tournent les martinets dans les hauteurs de l'air:
plus haut encore tournent les astres invisibles.
Que le jour se retire aux extrémités de la terre,
apparaîtront ces feux sur l'étendue de sombre sable . . .

Ainsi nous habitons un domaine de mouvements
et de distances; ainsi le coeur
va de l'arbre à l'oiseau, de l'oiseau aux astres lointains,
de l'astre à son amour. Ainsi l'amour
dans la maison fermée s'accroît, tourne et travaille,
serviteur des soucieux portant une lampe à la main.

PHILIPPE JACCOTTET (b. 1925)
translated by DEREK MAHON

The birds will still sing

Break my branches
saw me into bits
the birds will still sing
in my roots

Les oiseaux continuent à chanter

Abattez mes branches
sciez-moi en morceaux
les oiseaux continuent à chanter
dans mes racines

ANISE KOLTZ (b. 1928)
translated by JOHN MONTAGUE

$a$capitalist$

$a$capitalist$
$society$calculates$everything$
inmoneyandcapitalizesall
$services$everythingismonetarily$
$expressed$and$counted$precisely$
$everything$has$a$monetary$
$aspect$everythinghasa$
$monetary$smile$
$everything$

%et%kapitalistisk%

%et%kapitalistisk%
%samfund%beregner%alt%
%i%penge%og%kapitaliserer%alle%
%tjenstydelser%alt%får%pengemæssige%
%udtryk%alt%udregnes%nøje%
%alt%har%en%pengeside%
%alt%har%et%pengesmil%
%alting%

VAGN STEEN (b. 1928)
translated by the poet

From March '79

Tired of all who come with words, words but no language
I went to the snow-covered island.
The wild does not have words.
The unwritten pages spread themselves out in all directions!
I come across the marks of roe-deer's hooves in the snow.
Language but no words.

Från Mars-79

Trött på alla som kommer med ord, ord men inget språk
for jag till den snötäckta ön.
Det vilda har inga ord.
De oskrivna sidorna breder ut sig åt alla håll!
Jag stöter på spåren av rådjursklövar i snön.
Språk men inga ord.

TOMAS TRANSTRÖMER (b. 1931)
translated by JOHN F. DEANE

Merlin

I will consider the outnumbering dead:
For they are the husks of what was rich seed.
Now, should they come together to be fed,
They would outstrip the locusts' covering tide.

Arthur, Elaine, Mordred; they are all gone
Among the raftered galleries of bone.
By the long barrows of Logres they are made one,
And over their city stands the pinnacled corn.

GEOFFREY HILL (b. 1932)

This Moment

A neighbourhood.
At dusk.

Things are getting ready
to happen
out of sight.

Stars and moths.
And rinds slanting around fruit.

But not yet.

One tree is black.
One window is yellow as butter.

A woman leans down to catch a child
who has run into her arms
this moment.

Stars rise.
Moths flutter.
Apples sweeten in the dark.

EAVAN BOLAND (b. 1944)

The Gateway

Now the heart sings with all its thousand voices
To hear this city of cells, my body, sing.
The tree through the stiff clay at long last forces
Its thin strong roots and taps the secret spring.

And the sweet waters without intermission
Climb to the tips of its green tenement;
The breasts have borne the grace of their possession,
The lips have felt the pressure of content.

Here I come home: in this expected country
They know my name and speak it with delight.
I am the dream and you my gates of entry,
The means by which I waken into light.

A. D. HOPE (1907–2000)

'I sing of a maiden' and 'I have a gentil cock' (see p. 100).
BL MS Sloane 2593, f.10b. By permission of The British Library Board.

'I sing of a maiden'

I sing of a maiden
that is makeles
King of all kings
to her son she chose

he came also still
there his mother was
as dew in April
that falleth on the grass

he came also still
to his mother's bower
as dew in April
that falleth on the flower

he came also still
there his mother lay
as dew in April
that falleth on the spray

mother and maiden
was never none but she
well may such a lady
God's mother be

ANON. (early 15th century)

makeles: matchless

'Thread suns'

Thread suns
above the grey-black wilderness.
A tree-
high thought
tunes in to light's pitch: there are
still songs to be sung on the other side
of mankind.

'Fadensonnen'

Fadensonnen
über der grauschwarzen Ödnis.
Ein baum-
hoher Gedanke
greift sich den Lichtton: es sind
noch Lieder zu singen jenseits
der Menschen.

PAUL CELAN (1920–70)
translated by MICHAEL HAMBURGER

Song
to Celia

Drink to me only with thine eyes,
  And I will pledge with mine;
Or leave a kiss but in the cup,
  And I'll not look for wine.
The thirst that from the soul doth rise
  Doth ask a drink divine;
But might I of Jove's nectar sup,
  I would not change for thine.

I sent thee late a rosy wreath,
  Not so much honouring thee
As giving it a hope that there
  It could not withered be.
But thou thereon didst only breathe,
  And sent'st it back to me;
Since when it grows, and smells, I swear,
  Not of itself, but thee.

BEN JONSON (1572–1637)

Father William

'You are old, father William,' the young man said,
  'And your hair is exceedingly white:
And yet you incessantly stand on your head –
  Do you think, at your age, it is right?'

'In my youth,' father William replied to his son,
  'I feared it *might* injure the brain:
But now that I'm perfectly sure I have none,
  Why, I do it again and again.'

'You are old,' said the youth, 'as I mentioned before,
  And have grown most uncommonly fat:
Yet you turned a back-somersault in at the door –
  Pray what is the reason of that?'

'In my youth,' said the sage, as he shook his gray locks,
  'I kept all my limbs very supple
By the use of this ointment, five shillings the box –
  Allow me to sell you a couple.'

'You are old,' said the youth, 'and your jaws are too weak
  For anything tougher than suet:
Yet you eat all the goose, with the bones and the beak –
  Pray, how did you manage to do it?'

'In my youth,' said the old man, 'I took to the law,
  And argued each case with my wife,
And *the muscular strength, which it gave to my jaw*,
  Has lasted the rest of my life.'

'You are old,' said the youth, 'one would hardly suppose
    That your eye was as steady as ever:
Yet you balanced an eel on the end of your nose –
    What made you so *awfully* clever?'

'I have answered three questions, and that is enough,'
    Said his father, 'don't give yourself airs!
'Do you think I can listen all day to such stuff?
    Be off, or I'll kick you down stairs!'

LEWIS CARROLL (1832–98)

Father William From the author's manuscript copy of *Alice's Adventures Under Ground*. By permission of The British Library Board.

Home-Thoughts, from Abroad

I

Oh, to be in England
Now that April's there,
And whoever wakes in England
Sees, some morning, unaware,
That the lowest boughs and the brushwood sheaf
Round the elm-tree bole are in tiny leaf,
While the chaffinch sings on the orchard bough
In England – now!

II

And after April, when May follows,
And the whitethroat builds, and all the swallows!
Hark, where my blossomed pear-tree in the hedge
Leans to the field and scatters on the clover
Blossoms and dewdrops – at the bent spray's edge –
That's the wise thrush; he sings each song twice over,
Lest you should think he never could recapture
The first fine careless rapture!
And though the fields look rough with hoary dew,
All will be gay when noontide wakes anew
The buttercups, the little children's dower
– Far brighter than this gaudy melon-flower!

ROBERT BROWNING (1812–89)

Fenland Station in Winter

The railway station in winter lies wide open on three sides;
A waiting mousetrap.
No creatures out in the hard fields,
The desert of blue-lipped ice.
The tracks tweeze the last thin train away,
Wipe it on the rim, and lose it.

The sky is bent so low now, the wind is horizontal.
It whittles the sky's undersurface to the pith,
Paring away a grey unwinding peel of snow.
A mean, needling flake rides the flat wind,
Picking the empty teeth of the trees,
Then falling, frantic, to gnaw at the setting earth,
Clinging there like a starving mouse's claws in velvet.

KATHERINE PIERPOINT (b. 1961)

Monopoly

We sat like slum landlords around the board
buying each other out with fake banknotes,
until we lost more than we could afford,
or ever hope to pay back. Now our seats
are empty – one by one we left the game
to play for real, at first completely lost
in this other world, its building sites, its rain;
but slowly learned the rules or made our own,
stayed out of jail and kept our noses clean.
And now there's only me – sole freeholder
of every empty office space in town,
and from the quayside I can count the cost
each low tide brings – the skeletons and rust
of boats, cars, hats, boots, iron, a terrier.

PAUL FARLEY (b. 1965)

Caedmon's Hymn

(7th century AD)

Now we must praise to the skies the Keeper of the
    heavenly kingdom,
The might of the Measurer, all he has in mind,
The work of the Father of Glory, of all manner
    of marvel,

Our eternal Master, the main mover.
It was he who first summoned up, on our behalf,
Heaven as a roof, the holy Maker.

Then this middle-earth, the Watcher over humankind,
Our eternal Master, would later assign
The precinct of men, the Lord Almighty.

from Bede's HISTORY

translated by PAUL MULDOON

Caedmon's Hymn   11th-century manuscript. By permission of
the Syndics of Cambridge University Library.

Anglo-Saxon Riddle

I'm a strange creature, for I satisfy women,
a service to the neighbours! No one suffers
at my hands except for my slayer.
I grow very tall, erect in a bed,
I'm hairy underneath. From time to time
a good-looking girl, the doughty daughter
of some churl dares to hold me,
grips my russet skin, robs me of my head
and puts me in the pantry. At once that girl
with plaited hair who has confined me
remembers our meeting. Her eye moistens.

from THE EXETER BOOK

ANON. (before 1000)
translated by KEVIN CROSSLEY-HOLLAND

Suggested answer: Onion

from **The General Prologue to The Canterbury Tales**

Whan that Aprill with his shoures soote
The droghte of March hath perced to the roote,
And bathed every veyne in swich licour
Of which vertu engendred is the flour;
Whan Zephirus eek with his sweete breeth
Inspired hath in every holt and heeth
The tendre croppes, and the yonge sonne
Hath in the Ram his half cours yronne,
And smale foweles maken melodye,
That slepen al the nyght with open eye
(So priketh hem nature in hir corages);
Thanne longen folk to goon on pilgrimages,
And palmeres for to seeken straunge strondes,
To ferne halwes, kowthe in sondry londes;
And specially from every shires ende
Of Engelond to Caunterbury they wende,
The holy blisful martir for to seke,
That hem hath holpen whan that they were seeke.

(lines 1–18)

GEOFFREY CHAUCER (1340?–1400)

Sonnet 116

Let me not to the marriage of true minds
Admit impediments; love is not love
Which alters when it alteration finds,
Or bends with the remover to remove.
O no, it is an ever-fixed mark,
That looks on tempests and is never shaken;
It is the star to every wand'ring bark
Whose worth's unknown, although his height be taken.
Love's not Time's fool, though rosy lips and cheeks
Within his bending sickle's compass come;
Love alters not with his brief hours and weeks,
But bears it out even to the edge of doom.
  If this be error and upon me proved,
  I never writ, nor no man ever loved.

WILLIAM SHAKESPEARE (1564–1616)

The Argument of His Book

I sing of Brooks, of Blossomes, Birds, and Bowers:
Of April, May, of June, and July-Flowers.
I sing of May-poles, Hock-carts, Wassails, Wakes,
Of Bride-grooms, Brides, and of their Bridall-cakes.
I write of Youth, of Love, and have Accesse
By these, to sing of cleanly-Wantonnesse.
I sing of Dewes, of Raines, and piece by piece
Of Balme, of Oyle, of Spice, and Amber-Greece.
I sing of Times trans-shifting; and I write
How Roses first came Red, and Lillies White.
I write of Groves, of Twilights, and I sing
The Court of Mab, and of the Fairie-King.
I write of Hell; I sing (and ever shall)
Of Heaven, and hope to have it after all.

ROBERT HERRICK (1591–1674)

Jerusalem

And did those feet in ancient time
Walk upon England's mountains green:
And was the holy Lamb of God
On England's pleasant pastures seen?

And did the Countenance Divine
Shine forth upon our clouded hills?
And was Jerusalem builded here,
Among these dark Satanic Mills?

Bring me my Bow of burning gold:
Bring me my Arrows of desire:
Bring me my Spear: O clouds unfold:
Bring me my Chariot of fire:

I will not cease from Mental Fight
Nor shall my Sword sleep in my hand:
Till we have built Jerusalem,
In England's green & pleasant Land.

WILLIAM BLAKE (1757–1827)

'I would to heaven that I were
so much clay'

I would to heaven that I were so much clay,
  As I am blood, bone, marrow, passion, feeling –
Because at least the past were passed away –
  And for the future – (but I write this reeling,
Having got drunk exceedingly today,
  So that I seem to stand upon the ceiling)
I say – the future is a serious matter –
And so – for God's sake – hock and soda water!

GEORGE GORDON, LORD BYRON (1788–1824)

Cancelled stanza, written on the back of the poet's
manuscript of *Don Juan*, Canto I.

from **Among School Children**

Labour is blossoming or dancing where
The body is not bruised to pleasure soul,
Nor beauty born out of its own despair,
Nor blear-eyed wisdom out of midnight oil.
O chestnut-tree, great-rooted blossomer,
Are you the leaf, the blossom or the bole?
O body swayed to music, O brightening glance,
How can we know the dancer from the dance?

W. B. YEATS (1865–1939)

Not Waving but Drowning

Nobody heard him, the dead man,
But still he lay moaning:
I was much further out than you thought
And not waving but drowning.

Poor chap, he always loved larking
And now he's dead
It must have been too cold for him his heart gave way,
They said.

Oh, no no no, it was too cold always
(Still the dead one lay moaning)
I was much too far out all my life
And not waving but drowning.

STEVIE SMITH (1902–71)

Self-portrait of Stevie Smith
From *Collected Poems of Stevie
Smith* (Penguin 20th Century
Classics). By permission of
James MacGibbon.

Map of the New World: Archipelagoes

At the end of this sentence, rain will begin.
At the rain's edge, a sail.

Slowly the sail will lose sight of islands;
into a mist will go the belief in harbours
of an entire race.

The ten-years war is finished.
Helen's hair, a grey cloud.
Troy, a white ashpit
by the drizzling sea.

The drizzle tightens like the strings of a harp.
A man with clouded eyes picks up the rain
and plucks the first line of the *Odyssey*.

DEREK WALCOTT (b. 1930)

After the Fall

Adam: Lady,
I've not had a moment's love
since I was expelled.
Let me in.

Eve: Lord,
I've not had a moment's rest
since I was a rib.
Put me back.

ANNE STEVENSON (b. 1933)

Quark

'Transcendental,' said the technician,
'to stumble on a quark that talks back.
I will become a mystagogue, initiate
punters into the wonder of it for cash.'
'Bollocks,' said the quark, from its aluminium
nacelle. 'I don't need no dodgy
crypto-human strategising my future.
Gonna down-size under the cocoplum
or champak, drink blue marimbas into
the sunset, and play with speaking quarklike
while I beflower the passing gravitons.'

JO SHAPCOTT (b. 1953)

'Loving the rituals'

Loving the rituals that keep men close,
Nature created means for friends apart:

pen, paper, ink, the alphabet,
signs for the distant and disconsolate heart.

PALLADAS (4th century AD)
translated by TONY HARRISON

Auld Lang Syne

Should auld acquaintance be forgot,
  And never brought to min'?
Should auld acquaintance be forgot,
  And days o' lang syne?

Chorus: For auld lang syne, my dear,
        For auld lang syne,
        We'll tak a cup o' kindness yet,
        For auld lang syne.

We twa hae run about the braes,
  And pu'd the gowans fine;
But we've wander'd mony a weary foot
  Sin auld lang syne.
    For auld, &c.

We twa hae paidl't i' the burn,
  From mornin sun till dine;
But seas between us braid hae roar'd
  Sin auld lang syne.
    For auld, &c.

And here's a hand, my trusty fiere,
  And gie's a hand o'thine;
And we'll tak a right guid willie-
waught,
  For auld lang syne.
    For auld, &c.

And surely ye'll be your pint-stowp,
  And surely I'll be mine;
And we'll tak a cup o' kindness yet
  For auld lang syne.
For auld, &c.

ROBERT BURNS (1759–96)

braes: slopes
gowans: daisies
fiere: friend
waught: a hearty draught

from St. Paul's Epistle to the Corinthians

When I was a child, I spake as a child, I understood
as a child, I imagined as a child. But as soon as I
was a man, I put away childishness.

Now we see in a glass, even in a dark speaking: but then
shall we see face to face. Now I know unperfectly:
but then shall I know even as I am known.

Now abideth faith, hope, and love, even these three: but
the chief of these is love.

(1 CORINTHIANS: 13. 11–13)

translated by WILLIAM TYNDALE (1484–1536)

from Lines written a few miles above Tintern Abbey

       For I have learned
To look on nature, not as in the hour
Of thoughtless youth; but hearing oftentimes
The still, sad music of humanity,
Nor harsh nor grating, though of ample power
To chasten and subdue. And I have felt
A presence that disturbs me with the joy
Of elevated thoughts; a sense sublime
Of something far more deeply interfused,
Whose dwelling is the light of setting suns,
And the round ocean and the living air,
And the blue sky, and in the mind of man:
A motion and a spirit, that impels
All thinking things, all objects of all thought;
And rolls through all things.

WILLIAM WORDSWORTH (1770–1850)

from In Memoriam

Ring out, wild bells, to the wild sky,
  The flying cloud, the frosty light:
  The year is dying in the night;
Ring out, wild bells, and let him die.

Ring out the old, ring in the new,
  Ring, happy bells, across the snow:
  The year is going, let him go;
Ring out the false, ring in the true.

Ring out the grief that saps the mind,
  For those that here we see no more;
  Ring out the feud of rich and poor,
Ring in redress to all mankind.

(CVI, stanzas 1–3)

ALFRED, LORD TENNYSON (1809–92)

'There came a Wind like a Bugle'

There came a Wind like a Bugle –
It quivered through the Grass
And a Green Chill upon the Heat
So ominous did pass
We barred the Windows and the Doors
As from an Emerald Ghost –
The Doom's electric Moccasin
That very instant passed –
On a strange Mob of panting Trees
And Fences fled away
And Rivers where the Houses ran
Those looked that lived – that Day –
The Bell within the steeple wild
The flying tidings told –
How much can come
And much can go,
And yet abide the World!

EMILY DICKINSON (1830–86)

First Fig

My candle burns at both ends;
  It will not last the night;
But ah! my foes, and oh, my friends –
  It gives a lovely light!

EDNA ST. VINCENT MILLAY (1892–1950)

Song

Summer is over upon the sea.
The pleasure yacht, the social being,
that danced on the endless polished floor,
stepped and side-stepped like Fred Astaire,
is gone, is gone, docked somewhere ashore.

The friends have left, the sea is bare
that was strewn with floating, fresh green weeds.
Only the rusty-sided freighters
go past the moon's marketless craters
and the stars are the only ships of pleasure.

ELIZABETH BISHOP (1911–79)

Naima

for John Coltrane

Propped against the crowded bar
he pours into the curved and silver horn
his old unhappy longing for a home

the dancers twist and turn
he leans and wishes he could burn
his memories to ashes like some old notorious emperor

of rome. but no stars blazed across the sky when he
   was born
no wise men found his hovel. this crowded bar
   where dancers twist and turn

holds all the fame and recognition he will ever earn
on earth or heaven. he leans against the bar
and pours his old unhappy longing in the saxophone

KAMAU BRATHWAITE (b. 1930)

Season

Rust is ripeness, rust,
And the wilted corn-plume;
Pollen is mating-time when swallows
Weave a dance
Of feathered arrows
Thread corn-stalks in winged
Streaks of light. And, we loved to hear
Spliced phrases of the wind, to hear
Rasps in the field, where corn-leaves
Pierce like bamboo slivers.

Now, garnerers we
Awaiting rust on tassels, draw
Long shadows from the dusk, wreathe
Dry thatch in wood-smoke. Laden stalks
Ride the germ's decay – we await
The promise of the rust.

WOLE SOYINKA (b. 1935)

Prayer

Some days, although we cannot pray, a prayer
utters itself. So, a woman will lift
her head from the sieve of her hands and stare
at the minims sung by a tree, a sudden gift.

Some nights, although we are faithless, the truth
enters our hearts, that small familiar pain;
then a man will stand stock-still, hearing his youth
in the distant Latin chanting of a train.

Pray for us now. Grade I piano scales
console the lodger looking out across
a Midlands town. Then dusk, and someone calls
a child's name as though they named their loss.

Darkness outside. Inside, the radio's prayer –
Rockall. Malin. Dogger. Finisterre.

CAROL ANN DUFFY (b. 1955)

Season Song

'Sćel lem dúib'

Here's a song –
stags give tongue
winter snows
summer goes.

High cold blow
sun is low
brief his day
seas give spray.

Fern clumps redden
shapes are hidden
wildgeese raise
wonted cries.

Cold now girds
wings of birds
icy time –
that's my rime.

ANON. (9th century)

translated from the Irish by FLANN O'BRIEN

'No man is an island'

No man is an island, entire of itself; every man is a piece of the continent, a part of the main.

If a clod be washed away by the sea, Europe is the less, as well as if a promontory were, as well as if a manor of thy friend's or of thine own were.

Any man's death diminishes me, because I am involved in mankind. And therefore never send to know for whom the bell tolls; it tolls for thee.

from MEDITATION 17,
DEVOTIONS UPON EMERGENT OCCASIONS

JOHN DONNE (1572–1631)

A Song

Lying is an occupation
  Used by all who mean to rise;
Politicians owe their station
  But to well-concerted lies.

These to lovers give assistance,
  To ensnare the fair one's heart;
And the virgin's best resistance
  Yields to this commanding art.

Study this superior science,
  Would you rise in church or state;
Bid to truth a bold defiance,
  'Tis the practice of the great.

LAETITIA PILKINGTON (1708–50)

Chorus from Hellas

The world's great age begins anew,
  The golden years return,
The earth doth like a snake renew
  Her winter weeds outworn:
Heaven smiles, and faiths and empires gleam,
Like wrecks of a dissolving dream.

A brighter Hellas rears its mountains
  From waves serener far;
A new Peneus rolls his fountains
  Against the morning star.
Where fairer Tempes bloom, there sleep
Young Cyclads on a sunnier deep.

A loftier Argo cleaves the main,
  Fraught with a later prize;
Another Orpheus sings again,
  And loves, and weeps, and dies.
A new Ulysses leaves once more
Calypso for his native shore...

PERCY BYSSHE SHELLEY (1792–1822)

Return to Cornwall

I think no longer of the antique city
  Of Pompey and the red-haired Alexander.
The brilliant harbour, the wrecked light at Pharos,
  Are buried deep with Mediterranean plunder.

Here, by the Inney, nature has her city:
  (O the cypress trees of Mahomed Ali Square!)
The children build their harbour in the meadow
  And the crystal lark floats on the Cornish air.

CHARLES CAUSLEY (1917–2003)

True Stories (1)

Don't ask for the true story;
why do you need it?

It's not what I set out with
or what I carry.

What I'm sailing with,
a knife, blue fire,

luck, a few good words
that still work, and the tide.

MARGARET ATWOOD (b. 1939)

Guinep

Our mothers have a thing
about guinep:

Mind you don't eat guinep in your good clothes.
It will stain them.

Mind you don't climb guinep tree.
You will fall.

Mind you don't swallow guinep seed.
It will grow inside you.

Our mothers have a thing
about guinep: they're
secretly consuming it.

OLIVE SENIOR (b. 1943)

Guinep Illustration
by permission of the
Natural History
Museum.

Road

Traveller, your footprints are
the only path, the only track:
wayfarer, there is no way,
there is no map or Northern star,
just a blank page and a starless dark;
and should you turn round to admire
the distance that you've made today
the road will billow into dust.
No way on and no way back,
there is no way, my comrade: trust
your own quick step, the end's delay,
the vanished trail of your own wake,
wayfarer, sea-walker, Christ.

DON PATERSON (b. 1963)

from **Beowulf**

Then a powerful demon, a prowler through the dark,
nursed a hard grievance. It harrowed him
to hear the din of the loud banquet
every day in the hall, the harp being struck
and the clear song of a skilled poet
telling with mastery of man's beginnings,
how the Almighty had made the earth
a gleaming plain girdled with waters;
in His splendour He set the sun and the moon
to be earth's lamplight, lanterns for men,
and filled the broad lap of the world
with branches and leaves; and quickened life
in every other thing that moved.

(lines 86–98)

ANON. (10th century or earlier)
translated by SEAMUS HEANEY

For Pero Moniz, who died at sea

On earth I lived few years, and weary ones,
cram-full of stubborn, wretched misery;
the dark day's light deserted me so soon
I never saw my quarter century.

I travelled across far-off lands and seas
seeking some remedy for life, some cure;
but daring deeds do not bring happiness
to one who, finally, has no desire.

Portugal bred me in my dear and green
homeland of Alenquer; but corrupt air
trapped in my vessel, in this blood and bone,

made me a morsel for your fish, cruel
sea, breaking on barren Abyssinia
so distant from my fertile native soil.

———————

No mundo, poucos anos e cansados
vivi, cheios de vil miséria dura;
foi-me tão cedo a luz do dia escura
que não vi cinco lustros acabados.

Corri terras e mares apartados,
buscando à vida algum remédio ou cura;
mas aquilo que, enfim, não quer ventura,
não o alcançam trabalhos arriscados.

Criou-me Portugal na verde e cara
pátria minha Alenquer; mas ar corruto,
que neste meu terreno vaso tinha,

me fez manjar de peixes em ti, bruto
mar, que bates na Abássia fera e avara,
tão longe da ditosa pátria minha!

LUÍS DE CAMÕES (1524–80)
English version by PAUL HYLAND

Cradle Song

Golden slumbers kiss your eyes,
Smiles awake you when you rise;
Sleep, pretty wantons, do not cry,
And I will sing a lullaby,
Rock them, rock them, lullaby.

Care is heavy, therefore sleep you,
You are care, and care must keep you;
Sleep, pretty wantons, do not cry,
And I will sing a lullaby,
Rock them, rock them, lullaby.

THOMAS DEKKER (1570–1632)

Eternity

He who binds to himself a joy
Does the winged life destroy
But he who kisses the joy as it flies
Lives in Eternity's sun rise

WILLIAM BLAKE (1757–1827)

The Catch

Forget
the long, smouldering
afternoon. It is

this moment
when the ball scoots
off the edge

of the bat; upwards,
backwards, falling
seemingly

beyond him
yet he reaches
and picks it

out
of its loop
like

an apple
from a branch,
the first of the season.

SIMON ARMITAGE (b. 1963)

Sunrise Sequence

The day breaks – the first rays of the rising Sun, stretching
    her arms.
Daylight breaking, as the Sun rises to her feet.
Sun rising, scattering the darkness; lighting up the land...
With disc shining, bringing daylight, as the birds whistle
    and call...
People are moving about, talking, feeling the warmth.
Burning through the Gorge, she rises, walking westwards,
Wearing her waist-band of human hair.
She shines on the blossoming coolibah-tree, with its
    sprawling roots,
Its shady branches spreading...

from THE DULNGULG SONG CYCLE

translated by RONALD M. BERNDT

Mountain

Eastward, Mount Budawang
deliberately releases
stars, moon and sun
upward by night or day, one following one;

or rolls out nightly
and daily back again
a scroll and screen of cloud.

By dawn or twilight
it cuts a fine dark figure on the sky –
a lengthened strip of black calligraphy.

JUDITH WRIGHT (1915–2000)

Nasturtium Scanned

Ropey, lippy, loopy, scribbly
over a brick's edge,
she's a riot,
straggly as random and tricky as a diet,
tiddly, wobbly, oddly nibbly
and flashy as a landmine on her vine-meandrine
Alexandrine tangle-scanned line.

JUDITH RODRIGUEZ (b. 1936)

from The Vision of Piers Plowman

'After sharp showers,' said Peace, 'the sun shines brightest;
No weather is warmer than after watery clouds;
Nor any love dearer, or more loving friends,
Than after war and woe, when Love and Peace are masters.
There was never war in this world, or wickedness so keen,
That Love, if he liked, could not turn to laughter,
And Peace, through patience, put an end to all perils.'

(Passus 18, lines 413–17)

WILLIAM LANGLAND (*c.* 1332–1400)

'Fear no more the heat o' the sun'

Fear no more the heat o' the sun,
    Nor the furious winter's rages;
Thou thy worldly task hast done,
    Home art gone, and ta'en thy wages.
Golden lads and girls all must,
As chimney-sweepers, come to dust.

Fear no more the frown o' the great;
    Thou art past the tyrant's stroke;
Care no more to clothe and eat;
    To thee the reed is as the oak.
The sceptre, learning, physic, must
All follow this, and come to dust.

Fear no more the lightning flash,
    Nor th' all-dreaded thunder stone;
Fear not slander, censure rash;
    Thou hast finished joy and moan.
All lovers young, all lovers must
Consign to thee, and come to dust.

No exorciser harm thee!
Nor no witchcraft charm thee!
Ghost unlaid forbear thee!
Nothing ill come near thee!
Quiet consummation have;
And renowned be thy grave!

from CYMBELINE

WILLIAM SHAKESPEARE (1564–1616)

Sea Love

Tide be runnin' the great world over:
  'Twas only last June month I mind that we
Was thinkin' the toss and the call in the breast of the lover
  So everlastin' as the sea.

Heer's the same little fishes that sputter and swim,
  Wi' the moon's old glim on the grey, wet sand;
An' him no more to me nor me to him
  Than the wind goin' over my hand.

CHARLOTTE MEW (1869–1928)

To My Daughter

Bright clasp of her whole hand around my finger
My daughter, as we walk together now.
All my life I'll feel a ring invisibly
Circle this bone with shining: when she is grown
Far from today as her eyes are far already.

STEPHEN SPENDER (1909–95)

Thaw

The season midnight: glass
cracks with cold. From lighted shop-windows

girls half-sleeping, numb with frost step out.
We warm their hands between our hands, we kiss them

awake, and the planets
melt on their cheeks.

First touch, first tears. Behind their blue eyes darkness
shatters its pane of ice. We

step through into a forest
of sunlight, sunflowers.

DAVID MALOUF (b. 1934)

Epilogue

I have crossed an ocean
I have lost my tongue
from the root of the old one
a new one has sprung

GRACE NICHOLS (b. 1950)

Night Caller

Rain rains at half one in the morning and
the take-away stays open. My window is puddles
on pavements shimmering in street-lamp light.
In my hand the phone talks on; rain taps glass,
and running water runs to the ground.

Someone skids and screams their brakes a block away.

A silent film plays in the take-away across the
street. The traffic sounds like wind moving
round houses, and distant club-beats mud the
air and heave the city high.

The phone still speaks, the windy traffic blows,
The window runs. He talks like rain rains.
I listen like the take-away stays open.

LUCY POGSON

The Flags

Ships reflected on the waves
are flags of countries yet unknown
whose borders are identified
by sunlight on the pavingstone.

Unfurl the flag. Go on. Unfurl
the bridge bands on the river-skin
the battle-ships and towers in
the melted pearl

maybe a story, as well
that skims the water's upper-edge,
the walk beside the silver-dance
when the light is on the Thames.

MATTHEW PASKINS

I Think My Brain Is Coming Out of My Ears

Found a pink wet thing
like a prawn on my pillow this morning
felt it, smelt it, looked at it under the microscope
and I could see memories, rumours and dreams
scrawled in my handwriting over the surface.
I keep my bit of brain in a jar, feed it marmalade, call it Fred.
Frightening to think what might be missing –
unexplained chunks of life.
(I can't find the remote). Tonight
I sleep, orifices stuffed
and my ears glued to the sides of my head.

LUKE YATES

from The World

I saw Eternity the other night
Like a great Ring of pure and endless light,
    All calm, as it was bright,
And round beneath it, Time in hours, days, years
        Driv'n by the spheres
Like a vast shadow mov'd, in which the world
    And all her train were hurl'd…

HENRY VAUGHAN (1621–95)

A Riddle

Legs I have got, yet seldom do I walk;
I backbite many, yet I never talk:
In secret places most I seek to hide me,
For he who feeds me never can abide me.

ANON. (18th century)

A Riddle The illustration from *Food for the Mind, or A New Riddle-Book* by 'John-the-Giant-Killer, Esq.' (London, 1778).

February – not everywhere

Such days, when trees run downwind,
their arms stretched before them.

Such days, when the sun's in a drawer
and the drawer locked.

When the meadow is dead, is a carpet,
thin and shabby, with no pattern

and at bus stops people retract into collars
their faces like fists.

– And when, in a firelit room, a mother looks
at her four seasons, at her little boy,

in the centre of everything, with still pools
of shadows and a fire throwing flowers.

NORMAN MacCAIG (1910–96)

Peace (after Goethe)

For this, the dark, the ceasing of the winds
And the sky's gift, the steady rain,
And ours to one another, our bodies' happiness,
How in an after-life
We should hunger, thirst
And walk the many mansions grieving for this,
Our lying quiet. Therefore,
Sweet death, give us oblivion.

DAVID CONSTANTINE (b. 1944)

Wandrers Nachtlied

Der du von dem Himmel bist,
Alles Leid und Schmerzen stillest,
Den, der doppelt elend ist,
Doppelt mit Erquickung füllest,
Ach, ich bin des Treibens müde!
Was soll all der Schmerz und Lust?
Süsser Friede,
Komm, ach komm in meine Brust!

J. W. VON GOETHE (1749–1832)

The Present

For the present there is just one moon,
though every level pond gives back another.

But the bright disc shining in the black lagoon,
perceived by astrophysicist and lover,

is milliseconds old. And even that light's
seven minutes older than its source.

And the stars we think we see on moonless nights
are long extinguished. And, of course,

this very moment, as you read this line,
is literally gone before you know it.

Forget the here-and-now. We have no time
but this device of wantonness and wit.

Make me this present then: your hand in mine,
and we'll live out our lives in it.

MICHAEL DONAGHY (b. 1954)

Seed

The first warm day of spring
and I step out into the garden from the gloom
of a house where hope had died
to tally the storm damage, to seek what may
have survived. And finding some forgotten
lupins I'd sown from seed last autumn
holding in their fingers a raindrop each
like a peace offering, or a promise,
I am suddenly grateful and would
offer a prayer if I believed in God.
But not believing, I bless the power of seed,
its casual, useful persistence,
and bless the power of sun,
its conspiracy with the underground,
and thank my stars the winter's ended.

PAULA MEEHAN (b. 1955)

What He Said

What could my mother be
to yours? What kin is my father
to yours anyway? And how
did you and I meet ever?
                But in love
our hearts have mingled
like red earth and pouring rain.

CEMPULAPPEYANIRAR
(1st–3rd century AD)
translated by A. K. RAMANUJAN

What He Said A traditional Tamil
design. By permission of Gowri
Ramnarayan.

The Maiden's Song

When I was in my mother's bower
I had all that I would

The bailey beareth the bell away
The lily, the rose, the rose I lay

The silver is white, red is the gold
The robes they lay in fold

The bailey beareth the bell away
The lily, the rose, the rose I lay

And through the glass window shines the sun
How should I love and I so young

The bailey beareth the bell away
The lily, the rose, the rose I lay
The bailey beareth the bell away

ANON. (16th century)

The Maiden's Song The unique manuscript source of this anonymous Elizabethan song. BL Harley 7578, f. 110–110v. By permission of the British Library Board.

On a General Election

The accursèd power which stands on Privilege
(And goes with Women, and Champagne and Bridge)
Broke – and Democracy resumed her reign:
(Which goes with Bridge, and Women and Champagne).

HILAIRE BELLOC (1870–1953)

from The Mind Is An Ancient and Famous Capital

The mind is a city like London,
Smoky and populous: it is a capital
Like Rome, ruined and eternal,
Marked by the monuments which no one
Now remembers. For the mind, like Rome, contains
Catacombs, aqueducts, amphitheatres, palaces,
Churches and equestrian statues, fallen, broken or soiled.
The mind possesses and is possessed by all the ruins
Of every haunted, hunted generation's celebration...

DELMORE SCHWARTZ (1913–66)

Misty

How I love

The darkwave music
Of a sun's eclipse
You can't see for cloud

The saxophonist playing 'Misty'
In the High Street outside Barclays

Accompanied by mating-calls
Sparked off
In a Jaguar alarm

The way you're always there
Where I'm thinking

Or several beats ahead.

RUTH PADEL (b. 1947)

A Private Life

I want to drive home in the dusk
of some late afternoon,

the journey slow, the tractors spilling hay,
the land immense and bright, like memory,

the pit towns smudges of graphite,
their names scratched out for good: Lumphinnans;

Kelty. I want to see
the darkened rooms, the cups and wireless sets,

the crimson lamps across the playing fields,
the soft men walking home through streets and parks

and quiet women, coming to their doors,
then turning away, their struck lives gathered around them.

JOHN BURNSIDE (b. 1955)

Sonnet 73

That time of year thou mayst in me behold
When yellow leaves, or none, or few, do hang
Upon those boughs which shake against the cold,
Bare ruined choirs, where late the sweet birds sang.
In me thou seest the twilight of such day
As after sunset fadeth in the west;
Which by and by black night doth take away,
Death's second self, that seals up all in rest.
In me thou seest the glowing of such fire,
That on the ashes of his youth doth lie,
As the deathbed whereon it must expire,
Consumed with that which it was nourished by.
   This thou perceiv'st, which makes thy love more strong,
   To love that well, which thou must leave ere long.

WILLIAM SHAKESPEARE (1564–1616)

Grass

Pile the bodies high at Austerlitz and Waterloo.
Shovel them under and let me work –
      I am the grass; I cover all.

And pile them high at Gettysburg
And pile them high at Ypres and Verdun.
Shovel them under and let me work.
Two years, ten years, and passengers ask the conductor:
      What place is this?
      Where are we now?

      I am the grass.
      Let me work.

CARL SANDBURG (1878–1967)

The Sunflower

Bring me the sunflower and I'll transplant
it in my garden's burnt salinity.
All day its heliocentric gold face
will turn towards the blue of sky and sea.

Things out of darkness incline to the light,
colours flow into music and ascend,
and in that act consume themselves, to burn
is both a revelation and an end.

Bring me that flower whose one aspiration
is to salute the blond shimmering height
where all matter's transformed into essence,
its radial clockface feeding on the light.

Portami il girasole ch'io lo trapianti
nel mio terreno bruciato dal salino,
e mostri tutto il giorno agli azzurri specchianti
del cielo l'ansietà del suo volto giallino.

Tendono alla chiarità le cose oscure,
si esauriscono i corpi in un fluire
di tinte: queste in musiche. Svanire
è dunque la ventura delle venture.

Portami tu la pianta che conduce
dove sorgono bionde trasparenze
e vapora la vita quale essenza;
portami il girasole impazzito di luce.

EUGENIO MONTALE (1889–1981)
English version by JEREMY REED

The Sunburst

Her first memory is of light all around her
As she sits among pillows on a patchwork quilt
Made out of uniforms, coat linings, petticoats,
Waistcoats, flannel shirts, ball gowns, by Mother
Or Grandmother, twenty stitches to every inch,
A flawless version of *World without End* or
Cathedral Window or a diamond pattern
That radiates from the smallest grey square
Until the sunburst fades into the calico.

MICHAEL LONGLEY (b. 1939)

Freight song

We were lying, the two of us
on a freight lift platform

which four angels were hoisting up,
their haloes journeying

little by little up to blue sky.
And you were stacked next to me

and I was stacked alongside you
like two symbiotic suitcases

with labels reading: The Twilit Sky.
Our sleepy lift attendants

were the stars of heaven.
And we were the goods –

JUDITH KAZANTZIS (b. 1940)

NOTES TO THE POEMS

25   **Up in the Morning Early**   'The chorus of this song is old; the two stanzas are mine' (Burns's note).

33   **The Trees**   Philip Larkin was on the Arts Council committee when it approved a grant which enabled us to pay for the first year of advertising spaces on the Underground. He took a special interest in the project and wrote to us with useful suggestions: 'I have always liked the Wayside Pulpit placards ("Don't Put Your Wishbone Where Your Backbone Ought To Be"), and think it might be equally inspiring to be able to read on a tube journey poems that served as a reminder that the world of the imagination existed...What level of appreciation are you aiming at? Somerset Maugham, in his play-writing days, said that if you saw the audiences' taste in terms of the alphabet, it was best to aim at letter O. I don't think it would hurt to remind people of poems they already know; not everyone will know them.' Shortly before his death, he wrote to us again: 'I am glad your project is being favourably regarded; it makes me wonder whether I shall ever actually see one of the poems in the proposed location.' Sadly, he died before the first set of poems was posted.

35   **The Sick Rose**   William Blake, known in his own day as an engraver rather than a poet, published his *Songs of Innocence* and *Songs of Experience* in hand-engraved, hand-coloured editions of his own design ('illuminated printing'). This meant, in effect, that the poems remained virtually unknown until Blake was rediscovered as a great visionary poet in the 1860s. Both 'The Sick Rose' and 'The Tyger' were published in *Songs of Experience* (1794).

37   **At Lord's**   Cricket's laureate is Francis Thompson, whose 'At Lord's' evokes the image of an exiled Lancastrian watching a match at Lord's cricket ground but seeing in his mind's eye a game played elsewhere, many years before. The poem is a reduced version of a longer poem which mentions, as well as the Lancashire batsmen Hornby and Barlow, Gloucestershire's 'resistless' Grace brothers. When the poster appeared on the Tube, the former cricketer Mike Selvey reprinted it

331

in full in his *Guardian* Cricket Diary ('No, this isn't the arts page – just a bit of our cultural heritage for a change') and we were inundated with requests for the poem, mostly from Lancashire.

41   **Composed Upon Westminster Bridge**   'Written on the roof of a coach, on my way to France' (Wordsworth's note). With Wordsworth's dating of the poem in mind, we arranged a 'workshop' on Westminster Bridge at dawn on 3 September 1986. We advertised in the London listings magazines and to our amazement between twenty and thirty people turned up, including a visiting American professor and the poet Wendy Cope. At dawn (twelve minutes past six, BST) we read the poem aloud. Then we settled down to watch the sun rise and write some poems of our own. Aware that the Thames crosses England from west to east, we gazed downstream, waiting to see the sun. We might have waited a very long time, as on this stretch the Thames runs due north (towards Islington, York and the Arctic circle). In any case, it was an overcast morning. When the sun suddenly gleamed through, apparently to our south, we were mightily surprised. Once we were cold enough, we adjourned to a local coffee shop to warm up and read our poems.

When T. S. Eliot's 'Prelude' was displayed on the Tube, we held a second 'winter' workshop at dusk on Waterloo Bridge, somewhat impeded by rain and sleet.

43   **The Loch Ness Monster's Song**   The author explained in conversation that the lonely monster rises from the loch and looks round for the companions of his youth – prehistoric reptiles – and, finding nobody he knows, he descends again to the depths after a brief swearing session.

Some years ago, Edwin Morgan was commissioned by the Scottish Arts Council to write a series of poems for the inauguration of Glasgow's refurbished Underground system. He sent us this sample, which sent such alarm through the Strathclyde transport executive that they decided against using the poems.

The Subway Piranhas

Did anyone tell you
that in each subway train
there is one special seat

---

with a small hole in it
and underneath the seat
is a tank of piranha-fish
which have not been fed
for quite some time.
The fish become agitated
by the shoogling of the train
and jump up through the seat.
The resulting skeletons
of unlucky passengers
turn an honest penny
for the transport executive,
hanging far and wide
in medical schools.

44 **Living**   On learning that a poem of hers was to appear on the Underground, Denise Levertov, who was born in London but lived mainly in the United States, wrote to us: 'I am totally thrilled at the idea of having a poem in the Tube. I spent innumerable hours in the Tube from age 12–23, and a good many before and since, too. I am in fact a sort of Tube Rat, like a "rat" of the Paris Opera – a *denizen*. Appearance in American trains and buses means little to me – but London, ah, London! – that's different.'

49 **I Am Becoming My Mother**   The title poem of a volume for which Lorna Goodison was awarded the Commonwealth Poetry Prize (Americas region) for 1986.

50 **'Tagus farewell'**   Written in June 1539 in Spain, where Wyatt was Ambassador at the court of Charles V. Wyatt had just been recalled to London by Henry VIII, and the last lines of the poem may reflect some uneasiness at the fate awaiting him at home. The Spanish and Portuguese River Tagus is famous for its gold. Brutus, a descendant of Aeneas, dreamed that he was destined to found a kingdom in Albion.

53 **Lines** *from* **Endymion**   The famous opening lines of a long poem, and the first of a number of extracts in our collection.

54 **Goodbye**   Charlie Parker was an American jazz saxophonist, possibly the greatest of them all, who died in 1955, aged thirty-four.

---

57   **'So we'll go no more a-roving'**   Written in a letter to Thomas Moore in which Byron admits to over-indulging in carnival festivities: 'The mumming closed with a masked ball at the Fenice, where I went, as also to most of the ridottos, etc., etc., and, though I did not dissipate much upon the whole, yet I find "the sword wearing out the scabbard", though I have but just turned the corner of twenty-nine.'

71   **The Coming of Grendel**   Another extract. In this passage from the Old English epic, the monster Grendel (the original inhabitant of the land) closes in on the glittering wine-hall of the colonisers, where he means to wreak terrible havoc. The translation tries to be as literal as possible, while keeping the linguistic feeling of the original, with its resounding alliteration.

73   **Sonnet from the Portuguese**   The sonnets have no Portuguese original; they were written in secret the year before the poet's marriage to Robert Browning and tell the story of their unfolding love. In a letter to Leigh Hunt, Robert Browning explained how he persuaded Elizabeth Barrett Browning to publish these intimate poems: 'I never suspected the existence of those "Sonnets from the Portuguese" till three years after they were written. They were shown to me in consequence of some word of mine, just as they had been suppressed through some mistaken word; it was I who would not bear that sacrifice, and thought of the subterfuge of a name.' The sequence of forty-three sonnets appears as the final work in *Poems of Elizabeth Barrett Browning* (1850), immediately preceded by 'Catarina to Camoens' – a love poem addressed by his dying mistress to the great 16th-century Portuguese poet. The poems quickly became among the most celebrated love poems in the English language.

77   **Symphony in Yellow**   The sketch of Wilde was formerly attributed to Whistler, rather than to his wife, Beatrice. They were friends and neighbours of Wilde's in Tite Street, Chelsea.

79   **'Sumer is icumen in'**   Robert Graves and Laura Riding comment in their paper 'On Anthologies': 'Every possible polite explanation is given in popular anthologies for *verteth* to distract attention from the poetic meaning that the buck, full of Spring grass, *farteth*, i.e. breaks wind.' Scholarly debate still rages on this question, but on balance we agree with Graves and Riding.

---

89   **Everything Changes**   For the Brecht original, see below, pp.348–9.

90   **Roundel** *from* **The Parliament of Fowls**   Sung by the assembled
birds at the end of the St. Valentine's Day festivities, when each bird
has been happily paired off with its mate. 'The note,' the narrator ex-
plains, 'imaked was in France' – home of courtly love, which Chaucer's
delicious poem gently parodies.

95   *from* **To the City of London**   The fourth stanza of a seven-stanza
'balade' recited during Christmas week, 1501, at a dinner held by the
Lord Mayor in honour of the visiting Scottish Ambassador. Usually
assumed to be the work of the Scottish poet William Dunbar, who was
in London at the time.

96   **On First Looking into Chapman's Homer**   Composed during
October 1816, at dawn, as Keats walked home to Southwark from
Clerkenwell, where he had been visiting his former schoolteacher
Charles Cowden Clarke. They had stayed up all night reading Homer
in the magnificent translation of George Chapman.

100   **'I have a gentil cock'**   We have retained the old spelling of 'gentil'
to suggest 'gently bred' or 'aristocratic'. Chanticleer, in Chaucer's *Nun's
Priest's Tale*, is another 'gentil cock', described in similar terms:

> His coomb was redder than the fyn coral,
> And batailled as it were a castel wal;
> His byle was blak, and as the jeet it shoon,
> Lyk asure were his legges and his toon,
> His nayles whitter than the lylye flour,
> And lyk the burned gold was his colour.

103   **Mmenson**   *mmenson:* an orchestra of seven elephant tusk horns used
on state occasions to relate history; *Agades:* a town in the western
Sudan; *Sokoto:* a town in what is now northern Nigeria. (Notes by the
author.)

104   **Light**   Diane Wakoski felt that the extract from 'The Hitchhikers'
which originally appeared on the Underground would represent a
distortion of the poem if reproduced in a book, and we were happy
to substitute this complete short poem.

106 **'You took away all the oceans and all the room'** In 1934, after he was discovered to be the author of a bitter satire on Stalin, Mandelstam was arrested and exiled for three years, first to a small town in the Urals, then to the provincial town of Voronezh, where this poem was written. He was rearrested in 1938, and died en route to a labour camp.

110 **Old English Riddle** Suggested answer: *Bookworm*. This reminds us that bookworms have always been a genuine problem to book owners. This charming riddle is No. 47 in *The Exeter Book*, probably transcribed *c.* 960–70 by the first Bishop of Exeter. The riddles vary greatly in subject and style. Many are about the animal kingdom, others are about artefacts and yet others about the forces of nature – and there is a sprinkling of teasing double entendre, of a type still popular, which leads the reader to imagine two parallel solutions, one obscene, the other innocent (cf. p. 264).

118 **The Cries of London** Two stanzas of a broadside ballad in the 'Roxburghe Ballads', a unique collection of songs and ballads printed between 1560 and 1700, collected by Robert, Earl of Oxford, and now in the British Library. The 'cries' can be heard to this day in many traditional London markets.

122 **'Ich am of Irlonde'** Fragment of a medieval carol, written with other rhymes and doggerel in French and English on a single vellum leaf, now in the Bodleian Library, Oxford. W. B. Yeats uses the lines as a refrain for 'I am of Ireland', in *Words for Music Perhaps*:

> *'I am of Ireland,*
> *And the Holy Land of Ireland,*
> *And time runs on,' cried she.*
> *'Come out of charity,*
> *Come dance with me in Ireland.'*

126 **The Uncertainty of the Poet** 'The Tate Gallery yesterday announced that it had paid £1 million for a Giorgio de Chirico masterpiece, *The Uncertainty of the Poet*. It depicts a torso and a bunch of bananas' – *Guardian*, 2 April 1985. *With a Poet's Eye: A Tate Gallery Anthology*, for which the poem was first commissioned, presents paintings and poems side by side.

127 **'I saw a Peacock with a fiery tail'**   In his anthology *Come Hither* (1923), Walter de la Mare comments: 'So may the omission of a few commas effect a wonder in the imagination.' The first printing we were able to find was in *Westminster Drollery, Or, A Choice Collection of the Newest Songs and Poems both at Court and Theaters*, by A Person of Quality (1671). There the verse is headed: 'These following are to be understood two ways', and commas half-way through each line encourage the reader to pick up the double meaning. We have followed later editors in omitting the commas.

130 **On Himself**   The poet, who died in 1994, had been profoundly deaf since the age of seven, following an attack of scarlet fever. This poem appeared on the Underground in September 1991. A 1992 collection of David Wright's poems includes these moving lines:

An Appearance of Success

> Some verses, written when he was alive,
> A poster broadcast on the Underground;
> My life (an actor plays him) televised;
> Fame of a kind, if not recognition;
> Pleasing enough but not enough to please
> An unambitiousness at seventy-one,
> Or pierce the unawareness of the dead:
> This present I'd have loved to give to him
> To make amends,
> – My father – an appearance of success
> In his deaf difficult son;
> Something to recompense
> As may have seemed to him
> Rewardless and too long a sacrifice.

132 **The Passionate Shepherd to his Love**   Because of limited space, in our Underground poster we adapted the four-stanza version published in *The Passionate Pilgrim* (1599). The six-stanza version published in *England's Helicon* (1600) has been reprinted ever since in this form, often with its companion piece, 'The Nymph's Reply to the Shepherd' by Sir Walter Raleigh:

If all the world and love were young,
And truth in every shepherd's tongue,
These pretty pleasures might me move
To live with thee and be thy love.

Time drives the flocks from field to fold,
When rivers rage and rocks grow cold,
And Philomel becometh dumb;
The rest complains of cares to come.

The flowers do fade, and wanton fields
To wayward winter reckoning yields;
A honey tongue, a heart of gall,
Is fancy's spring, but sorrow's fall.

Thy gowns, thy shoes, thy beds of roses,
Thy cap, thy kirtle, and thy posies
Soon break, soon wither, soon forgotten, –
In folly ripe, in reason rotten.

Thy belt of straw and ivy buds,
Thy coral clasps, and amber studs,
All these in me no means can move
To come to thee and be thy love.

But could youth last and love still breed,
Had joys no date nor age no need,
Then these delights my mind might move
To live with thee and be thy love.

133 **Letter to André Billy**   During the First World War, Apollinaire served in the French artillery and infantry. He survived a skull wound towards the end of the war, but died a few months later in the influenza epidemic ravaging Paris. In a letter to his friend André Billy, he wrote of his *Calligrammes:* 'They are an idealization of *vers-libre* poetry and of typographical precision at a time when typography is brilliantly ending its career, at the dawn of new methods of reproduction, the cinema and the gramophone.' In the original French text, typography is used to suggest the shape of a bird of prey (as a shell), an eye, and a cathedral (specifically, Notre Dame).

Poème epistolaire

Premier canonnier conducteur
Je suis au front et te salue
Non non tu n'as pas la berlue
Cinquante-neuf est mon secteur

J'entends siffl
Le ^e^r l'oiseau
bel oiseau rap^a_{ce}

Je vois de lo_i_n
La cathédra^{le}

```
O    C
M    H
O    E
N A R
N D R E
B I L L Y
```

---

139 **To Emilia V –** Mary Shelley discovered these lines in one of Shelley's notebooks after his death, when she was transcribing his poems for publication. The manuscript draft which we reproduce, the only known source of the poem, was composed at the same time as the opening lines of *Epipsychidion*, Shelley's celebration of love. The same images appear in both texts: music, memory, rose leaves (or petals).

> Sweet Spirit! Sister of that orphan one,
> Whose empire is the name thou weepest on,
> In my heart's temple I suspend to thee
> These votive wreaths of withered memory.
>   Poor captive bird! who, from thy narrow cage,
> Pourest such music, that it might assuage
> The rugged hearts of those who prisoned thee,
> Were they not deaf to all sweet melody;
> This song shall be thy rose: its petals pale
> Are dead, indeed, my adored Nightingale!
> But soft and fragrant is the faded blossom,
> And it has no thorn left to wound thy bosom.
>
> (lines 1–12)

Emilia Viviani, to whom these lines were addressed, was the daughter of the Governor of Pisa. Shelley visited her in the convent where she was awaiting an arranged marriage, and he took a deep interest in her fate. She wrote sonnets and an essay on Love, a sentence of which Shelley uses as an epigraph to *Epipsychidion*. 'Music, when soft voices die' also pays a compliment to Emilia's writing, the 'thoughts' which, when their author is gone, Love itself shall slumber on.

142 **The Lobster Quadrille** From *Alice in Wonderland*. This poem, which parodies Mary Howitt's '"Will you walk into my Parlour?" said the spider to the fly', is sung to Alice by the Mock Turtle, while he and his friend the Gryphon 'solemnly' dance on the sea-shore.

144 **'I shall say what inordinate love is'** 'Inordinate' rather than lawful love is the subject of this lyric. In the original MS, the poem is accompanied by a briefer Latin original (which also appears elsewhere). The Latin treats merely of *Amor* (love), rather than the inordinate variety:

> Dicam quid sit Amor: Amor est insania mentis
> Ardor inextinctus, insaciata fames
> Dulce malum, mala dulcedo, dulcissimus error
> Absque labore quies, absque quiete labor.

Of the many English variations on this theme during the Renaissance, probably the most famous is Shakespeare's definition of 'lust' in Sonnet 129:

> Mad in pursuit, and in possession so;
> Had, having, and in quest to have, extreme;
> A bliss in proof, and proved, a very woe,
> Before, a joy proposed; behind, a dream.

145 **A red red Rose** Burns copied out a slightly different version of this song in a letter to his friend Alexander Cunningham, describing it as 'a simple old Scots song' which he had picked up in the country. Virtually every stanza of the song can be matched in oral tradition and earlier broadsheet ballads, and Burns's editors disagree on the extent to which he may have altered or improved it. But the final version seems unmistakably to have his special touch, in its tenderness and lyricism and its impeccable rhythms.

148 **To Someone Who Insisted I Look Up Someone** The American poet X. J. Kennedy wrote from Bedford, Massachusetts: 'What a

gleeful thing, to have lines perused by London straphangers (or is it pole-clingers?). Your picking that item delighted me more than if the Swedish Academy had handed me the Nobel Prize, and seemed about equally incredible.'

149 **Two Fragments** Sappho, the great lyric poet of the ancient world, called by Plato 'the Tenth Muse', was born in the late 7th century BC on the island of Lesbos. Much of her poetry has come to us from fragments of papyrus discovered in the late 19th century; other poems, including the two fragments translated here, were quoted by ancient grammarians.

150 **I Am** Written in Northampton County Asylum, this is the best-known of John Clare's many poems. After a brief period of fame as a 'peasant genius', Clare became more and more disorientated, and lived in mental asylums from 1837 until his death in 1864. The confusion from which he suffered did not affect his lucidity as a poet. He continued until the end to produce work of a high order.

151 **Dream Boogie** Langston Hughes, born in Joplin, Missouri, was a major figure in the Harlem Renaissance of the 1920s and '30s. 'Dream Boogie' is the first poem of *Montage of a Dream Deferred* (1951), a sequence of poems which use the idiom of bebop to portray the dreams of ordinary men and women in New York's Black ghetto.

155 **The Flaw in Paganism** Dorothy Parker, poet, journalist and short story writer, was one of the inner circle of wits and literary celebrities who met regularly for lunch at the Algonquin Hotel in New York in the 1920s. She worked in Hollywood as a scriptwriter, became involved in radical politics, and was blacklisted during the McCarthy period.

156 **Anthem for Doomed Youth** 'Above all I am not concerned with Poetry. My subject is War, and the pity of War. The Poetry is in the pity' (from Wilfred Owen's draft *Preface* to his war poems). Owen's poetical manifesto has an added poignancy since he was killed in France just seven days before the Armistice.

158 **A Picture** Bei Dao ('North Island') is the pen name of Zhao Zhenkai, a leading Chinese dissident writer. He was in Berlin at the time of the Tiananmen Square massacre (4 June 1989), and has lived in exile since then. He now lives in Davis, California, with the artist Shao Fei and their daughter Tiantian.

161 **'Gray goose and gander'** The origins of this fragment are unknown. Its first printing is in J. O. Halliwell's *Nursery Rhymes of England*, 3rd edition (1844).

162 **Sonnet: On His Blindness** Milton went totally blind in his early forties. In another sonnet on his blindness, written for his friend and pupil Cyriack Skinner, Milton explains that he lost his sight 'In liberty's defence' – that is, through writing his anti-clerical and political pamphlets, including *Areopagitica*, his eloquent plea for freedom of thought and the press.

164 **Late Summer Fires** The regeneration of land by setting fire to it is an ancient Aboriginal technique. Les Murray kindly wrote to us elucidating two phrases in the poem: 'The "hardcourt game" is life in Outback Australia, where soils tend to be pink to ochre to blood red and most often very hard and bare, under the cover of low bush ... So your note could say "hardcourt: refers to the hard red soils of inland Australia." And the Aboriginal flag (black and red, with a yellow disc at the centre), relates to that – the red once again standing for that soil and the blood spilt on it, while the black's for the people and the yellow disc is the sun.'

166 **The Twa Corbies** First printed in Sir Walter Scott, *Minstrelsy of the Scottish Border* (1802–3). Readers may like to compare the Scots border ballad with the popular English ballad **The Three Ravens**, first set to music by Thomas Ravenscroft in 1611:

> There were three Ravens sat on a tree,
> *Downe a downe, hay down, hay downe.*
> There were three Ravens sat on a tree,
> *With a downe.*
> There were three Ravens sat on a tree,
> They were as blacke as they might be.
> *With a downe derrie, derrie, derrie, downe, downe.*

The one of them said to his mate,
Where shall we our breakefast take?

Downe in yonder greene field,
There lies a Knight slain under his shield.

His hounds they lie downe at his feete,
So well they can their Master keepe.

His Haukes they flie so eagerly,
There's no fowle dare him come nie.

Downe there comes a fallow Doe,
As great with yong as she might goe.

She lift up his bloudy hed,
And kist his wounds that were so red.

She got him up upon her backe,
And carried him to earthen lake.

She buried him before the prime,
She was dead her selfe ere even-song time.

God send every gentleman
Such haukes, such hounds, and such a Leman.

167 **'The Great Frost'**   'Frost fairs' were held on the frozen Thames in the bitter winters of 1684 and 1698. John Evelyn described the extraordinary scene in his Diary, 24 January 1684: 'Coaches plied from Westminster to the Temple and from several other stairs to and fro, as in the streets, sleds, sliding with skates, a bull-baiting, horse and coach races, puppet plays and interludes, cooks, tippling and other lewd places, so that it seemed to be a Bacchanalian triumph, or carnival on the water.'

172 **A True and Faithful Inventory**   Printed in *Swift: Poetical Works*, edited by Herbert Davis (OUP 1967). Thomas Sheridan was an Irish schoolmaster, one of several friends with whom Swift liked to exchange puns, riddles and verse epistles.

174 **Thanks Forever**   The New York poet Milton Kessler was a good friend of the Editors, and an assiduous correspondent, often sending

us short poems based on his frequent London visits, like this one, typed on a postcard sent in 1990:

While Visiting You in '87

Having a bitter on the Thames:
Flat excursion ferries trailing the harbor master's wake.

'I don't want to get a call saying you've collapsed,' she said.
'You're just like an old tire about to burst,' he had said.

Look into your assymetrical pupils and don't worry
over the defect they reflect. And say,

'Just have a little bitter on the Thames.'

'Thanks Forever' is a contemporary view of a scene similar to that described by Walt Whitman in 'Crossing Brooklyn Ferry', in which the poet stands at the ferry rail imagining later generations standing at the same spot, gazing at the same river and sky. The first section of Whitman's poem celebrating his beloved city was displayed on the London Underground, alongside 'Thanks Forever', as part of an exchange of poems with the New York City Transit Authority.

183 **'Let my shadow disappear into yours'**   Our contribution to an exchange of poems with Stockholm Transport, which displayed Kipling's 'A Dead Statesman' at the same time, as part of a series of poems by Nobel Prize winners.

190 *from* **Requiem**   For seventeen months, the Russian poet Anna Akhmatova queued daily outside the prison in Leningrad where her son was held. This extract from *Requiem* is part of a cycle of poems that covers the years between 1935 and 1940 and commemorates the sufferings of ordinary men and women, victims of Stalin's purges.

191 **The Exiles**   From the time of the Highland Clearances until the early years of this century, famine and bitter poverty drove thousands of Highlanders to leave Scotland and emigrate to North America in search of a living. Iain Crichton Smith told us that the starting point for this poem was a visit he made to Canada, when he discovered many familiar Scottish place names.

---

193 **'My true love hath my heart and I have his'**   This famous lyric was first printed in this form by George Puttenham, *The Arte of English Poesie* (1589). Puttenham quotes the poem as an example of 'musicall ditties to be song to the lute or harpe', which suggests that it may have been set to music before 1589. The poem is a shortened version of a sonnet in Book Three of Sidney's *Arcadia*, written for his sister, Mary, Countess of Pembroke, when Sidney was in his early twenties.

198 **To My Dear and Loving Husband**   Anne Bradstreet grew up in the household of the Earl of Lincoln, where her father, Thomas Dudley, an ardent Puritan, was steward. In 1630, when she was eighteen, she emigrated to the Massachusetts Bay Colony with her husband Simon Bradstreet and her father, each of whom later became Governor of the colony. Her poems were published in England in 1650, as *The Tenth Muse Lately Sprung Up in America*.

199 **Chorus from a Play**   From *The Secular Masque*, one of the last works written by Dryden, in which he sums up a century riven by religious war.

200 **Inversnaid**   Dated September 28, 1881. Burn: a small river or stream. The Snaid burn runs from Loch Arklet to the tiny hamlet of Inversnaid, where it enters Loch Lomond. After seven weeks' service in the Glasgow slums as assistant at St Joseph's Church, Hopkins visited Loch Lomond and spent a few hours at Inversnaid. Several of the unfamiliar terms in the poem are his own coinage.

203 **His Return to London**   Having remained loyal to Charles I, Herrick was ejected in 1647 from his post as vicar at Dean Prior, Devon, and retired to London, where he remained until 1660. Several of Herrick's poems praise the simple pleasures of country life; he is best known as the poet who sings 'of Brooks, of Blossomes, Birds, and Bowers' (included in our 'A Thousand Years of Poetry in English', see p. 267). But his joy at escaping from Devon to London in 1647 is confirmed by an earlier poem, 'Discontents in Devon':

> More discontents I never had
>   Since I was born, than here;
> Where I have been, and still am sad,
>   In this dull Devonshire;

Yet justly too I must confess;
   I ne'er invented such
Ennobled numbers for the Press,
   Than where I loath'd so much.

211–13 Prizewinners, The TLS/Poems on the Underground Poetry Competition 1996 Our poetry competition on urban themes, sponsored and co-judged by *The Times Literary Supplement*, generated a mass of remarkable material from all parts of the UK and several countries abroad. Entries touched on every aspect of urban life, including praise of a city's history, despair at its decline, cheerful or apocalyptic predictions as to its future. Above all, it was the people of the city who were presented: shopkeepers, city gents, tramps and beggars, a Turkish barber, a Rasta bus-driver, gentle skinheads, transvestites, office cleaners, accountants, children, shoppers. Many poems were angry, dealing as they did with deprivation and poverty. But others were humane and full of optimism, as they drew attention to the great mix of cultures to be found in any large urban population – especially in London – and to the small pleasures of urban life, the glimpse of a fox, the delights of parks and open spaces and the river. It was difficult to choose three prizewinning poems out of so many of a high standard, and the ones we chose were not necessarily representative. But we thought each of them offered an original and imaginative glimpse of urban life, and we were delighted to offer them to the public in the final set of the year.

212 Potosí A silver-mining city in the mountains of Bolivia.

217 Nightsong: City First published in *Sirens Knuckles Boots* (1963), a collection that describes, with anger and eloquence, the evils of life under apartheid in South Africa. Dennis Brutus was born in Zimbabwe of South African parents, attended the University of Witwatersrand, and taught for fourteen years in South African high schools. He was arrested in 1963, and was sentenced to eighteen months' hard labour for his political activities. He has been a Professor of English at Northwestern University (Evanston, Illinois) and in the Africana Department, University of Pittsburgh.

220 Rondel Charles d'Orléans, the great French poet of courtly love, was born in Paris in 1394; he was nephew to the French king. At the age of twenty-one, he led the French forces at the battle of Agincourt, where he was taken prisoner (a scene immortalised in Shakespeare's *Henry V*). Charles was imprisoned in England for twenty-five years, a closely guarded hostage, well supplied with servants, French wine and writing materials. His poems in French and English are preserved in illustrated manuscripts in the British Library and the Bibliothèque Nationale, and have been widely anthologised. The 'rondel' printed here was displayed on the Paris Métro, in 'Des rimes en vers et en bleu' (a pun on the Métro colours), a programme displaying poems on stations and in trains, started in 1993. We commissioned a new translation by Oliver Bernard, with the support of an Arts Council Translation Grant.

223 **The Faun** A poem from an early collection of Verlaine's, *Fêtes galantes*, published in 1869 when the poet was twenty-five. These melancholy poems evoke the paintings of the early-18th-century artist Watteau, with elegant ladies and gentlemen drifting through an idealised landscape in pursuit of a doomed pleasure. John Montague's new translation was commissioned by us for Underground display, with support from the Arts Council of England.

229 **Harvestwoman** Fernando Pessoa is considered to be the greatest 20th-century Portuguese poet, but his poetry remains unfamiliar to most English readers, in spite of translations by Jonathan Griffin, Edwin Honig and, most recently, Keith Bosley. He wrote under several 'heteronyms', each with a different personality and style (Alberto Caeiro, Alvaro de Campos, Ricardo Reis), returning periodically to his own name and persona. He was active in launching several Modernist and Futurist journals, mostly short-lived, and he was haunted through his life by spells of depression and an acute sense of failure. Having lived as a child in South Africa, he wrote in English as well as Portuguese, and he knew English poetry intimately. 'Harvestwoman' and a longer poem on the same theme, translated by Keith Bosley as 'Poor reaper, she is singing, singing', suggest affinities with Wordworth's 'The Solitary Reaper' and Wallace Stevens's 'The Idea of Order at Key West':

> It was her voice that made
> The sky acutest at its vanishing.
> She measured to the hour its solitude.
> She was the single artificer of the world
> In which she sang. And when she sang, the sea,

Whatever self it had, became the self
That was her song, for she was the maker. Then we,
As we beheld her striding there alone,
Knew that there never was a world for her
Except the one she sang and, singing, made.

234 *from* **Dover Beach**   We were of two minds about whether to use the first section or the last of this oft-anthologised poem, which so beautifully expresses Victorian melancholy. As a compromise, we featured the opening lines on the Tube, and reprint both sections here.

238–52 **European Poems on the Underground**   The following poems were drawn from the fifteen countries of the European Union to mark the British EU presidency, with Geoffrey Hill representing the UK and Eavan Boland representing Ireland.

The poets featured are European in the widest sense. Cavafy, the supreme poet of homosexual love, was an Alexandrian Greek. The Finnish poet Edith Södergran, born in St. Petersburg and educated at a German academy, wrote her strange visionary poems in Swedish, introducing European modernism to Scandinavia. Alain Bosquet, self-styled 'censor, clown and sometime saboteur', was a citizen first of Belgium, then of France; he was born Anatoly Bisk in Odessa. His translator and friend Samuel Beckett is claimed equally by Ireland and France. The Luxembourg poet Anise Koltz, founding member with Alain Bosquet of the European Academy of Poetry, writes in three languages and has been translated into half a dozen more. Erich Fried, author of *100 Poems Without a Country*, fled Vienna in 1938 for London, where he continued to write in his native German. Taken together, the poems testify to the role of the poet in 20th-century European culture as a mediating force against the bitter sectarian and nationalistic violence which has defined the age.

The group of poems included one poem from an earlier set, 'Everything Changes' (see above, p. 89), with the Brecht original:

Alles wandelt sich. Neu beginnen
Kannst du mit dem letzten Atemzug.
Aber was geschehen, ist geschehen. Und das Wasser
Das du in den Wein gossest, kannst du
Nicht mehr herausschütten.

Was geschehen, ist geschehen. Das Wasser
Das du in den Wein gossest, kannst du
Nicht mehr herausschütten, aber
Alles wandelt sich. Neu beginnen
Kannst du mit dem letzten Atemzug.

243 **25 February 1944** 'Cf. Dante, *Inferno* III.57 ("che morte tanta n'avesse disfatta") and T. S. Eliot, "The Burial of the Dead", *The Waste Land*: "I had not thought death had undone so many."' (Note by P. L.) Towards the end of 1943, Primo Levi was captured with other Italian partisans and sent to a detention camp at Fossoli. On 22 February 1944 he was transported with 650 other Jews to Auschwitz. Of these, ninety-six men and twenty-nine women were 'saved' for the labour camps of Monowitz-Buna and Birkenau; the others went to the gas chambers. Only three of those who were 'saved' survived the war.

251 **Merlin** Logres (or Loegria): an ancient name for England. Merlin was the enchanter in Arthurian legends who appeared in stories of King Arthur, Elaine and the traitorous knight Mordred.

255 **'I sing of a maiden'** This gentle and numinous lyric comes from the same 15th-century notebook as 'I have a gentil cock' (p. 100). Scholars conjecture that the collection may have been compiled by a travelling musician for performance. The notebook, measuring 4½ by 6 inches, is the unique surviving source of about seventy-five medieval lyrics, including carols, love poems and drinking songs, all transcribed in a single hand. The manuscript is attributed to the monastery of Bury St. Edmunds, in West Suffolk, founded in the 11th century, though scholars assign the hand to the early 15th century. The lyrics probably go back fifty or a hundred years before.

256 **'Thread suns'** A second Austrian poem, part of an 'exchange' of poems between London and Vienna, marking the changeover of the EU presidency from Britain to Austria. Paul Celan was born into a Jewish family in Bukovina, a German enclave in Romania; his parents died in an internment camp, but he survived the war, later settling in Paris. His poems, like the writings of Primo Levi, are seared by the trauma of the Holocaust.

258 **Father William** We are using the first version, which comes from Lewis Carroll's hand-lettered manuscript of 1864, *Alice's Adventures*

Under Ground. The illustration is by Carroll himself. The poem is a parody of Robert Southey's moralistic verses, *The Old Man's Comforts and How He Gained Them*, which Alice Liddell, the Alice of the story, would certainly have known. We print below an example of the original Father William's responses.

> 'In the days of my youth,' Father William replied,
>   'I remembered that youth could not last;
> I thought of the future, whatever I did,
>   That I never might grieve for the past.'

263 **Caedmon's Hymn** Usually assumed to be the earliest extant poem in Old English, probably composed sometime between 658 and 680. In his *Ecclesiastical History of the English People* (completed 731), the Venerable Bede tells the story of an unlettered lay brother at Whitby who was granted the gift of song in a vision while he was guarding the stables. His hymn in praise of Creation is interpolated in the original Old English in several 8th-century Latin manuscripts of Bede's *History*. Paul Muldoon's new translation was commissioned by Poems on the Underground with support from the Arts Council Translation Fund.

274 **Quark** *Quark*: a sub-atomic particle (originally 'quork'), after *Finnegans Wake*: 'Three quarks for Muster Mark!' ('If quarks exist, they would represent a more fundamental building block of matter than any yet known', *The Observer*, 1967.) *Graviton*: a hypothetical sub-atomic particle.

275 **'Loving the rituals'** Palladas was an Alexandrian schoolmaster whose epigrams were collected in *The Greek Anthology*. According to Tony Harrison, Palladas' poems 'are the last hopeless blasts of the old Hellenistic world, giving way reluctantly, but without much resistance, before the cataclysm of Christianity'.

278 *from* **St. Paul's Epistle to the Corinthians** The publication of vernacular Bibles was a dangerous undertaking in the early 16th century. Inspired by the example of Luther's German version, the Protestant scholar, William Tyndale, resolved to produce a faithful English text that could be understood by readers without the intercession of the priesthood. Persecuted by the authorities, he fled to Germany

(where he met Luther) and continued his work there. Hundreds of copies of his New Testament were seized and burned. But the book survived. The quality of Tyndale's translation was such that the scholars who prepared the 1611 Authorised Version followed it closely. In 1536 Tyndale was arrested in Antwerp, found guilty of heresy and burnt at the stake.

276 **Auld Lang Syne** Not entirely by Burns, who claimed to have taken it down 'from an old man's singing'. The chorus had been in print for some time and the title is quoted by Allan Ramsay (1686–1758). It is probable, however, that the bulk of the verses, as we know them, are Burns's work.

284 **Naima** One of the best-loved works by the saxophonist John Coltrane, named after his first wife, and strongly influenced by non-Western harmonies and rhythms.

290 **Chorus from Hellas** Shelley composed *Hellas* in 1821, when the outcome of the Greek revolution was very much in doubt. His words were more prophetic than he knew: by 'another Orpheus' he probably meant Lord Byron, who died in Greece in 1824 on a mission to help the revolutionary forces.

293 **Guinep** A small, grape-like fruit with a green skin and a large seed surrounded by sweet, fleshy pulp. Guinep originally grew in Venezuela and was brought to the Caribbean islands by the Spanish conquerors.

294 **Road** Don Paterson's collection, *The Eyes*, pays tribute to the great Spanish poet Antonio Machado (1875–1939). 'Road' is inspired by a poem from Machado's *Proverbios y cantares*:

> Caminante, son tus huellas
> el camino, y nada más;
> caminante, no hay camino,
> se hace camino al andar…

295 *from* **Beowulf** The manuscript of this tremendous epic was 'lost' for nearly a thousand years. It was rediscovered in the 18th century

after a great library fire, and is now one of the treasures of the British Library, on permanent display in the Exhibition Rooms. This is our second extract (cf. p. 71 and Note), and comes from Seamus Heaney's vigorous and wonderfully readable translation of the entire work.

296 **For Pero Moniz, who died at sea** 'This sonnet, first published posthumously in 1598, is written in the voice of Camões's young comrade-in-arms Pero Moniz, from Alenquer near Torres Vedras in Portugal, who died in the Gulf of Aden. Some consider it the most beautiful of Camões's memorial poems because the poet sensed that his destiny paralleled his friend's so closely.' (P. H.). Commissioned by Poems on the Underground, with support from the Calouste Gulbenkian Foundation.

301–3 **Australian Poems on the Underground** A special display to mark the centenary of Australia's Treaty of Federation, supported by the Australian Tourist Commission and the Commonwealth Institute. Other Australian poets featured in our programme include A. D. Hope, Peter Porter, Les Murray and David Malouf.

304 *from* **The Vision of Piers Plowman** Our brief extract from *Piers Plowman*, one of the masterpieces of medieval English poetry, gives a taste of its message and its alliterative power. It is roughly contemporary with Chaucer's *Canterbury Tales*. Its forthright narration placed the common man on a par with the priesthood, and the satiric treatment of the corrupt clergy contributed to the social unrest that led to the Peasants' Revolt. The poem is attributed to William Langland, about whom little is known.

310–12 **Young Poets on the Underground** To end our celebration of a thousand years of poetry in English, we invited all prizewinners and runners-up in the Poetry Society's annual competition for young poets to submit short poems suitable for the Tube. Out of the excellent entries, we selected three poems for display, reprinted here.

316 **Peace (after Goethe)** 'I saw no way of translating Goethe's poem directly. Instead, I imagined the condition his poem prays for, and thought how unbearable it would be to look back on such peace and

well-being from any ghostly after-life. I kept to the same number of lines as Goethe used and imitated the syntax by which something necessary for our complete understanding is withheld until the last.' (D. C.). Commissioned by Poems on the Underground, with support from the Goethe Institute and the Arts Council of England. In addition to the poems by Goethe and David Constantine, the Tube poster included the British Library manuscript of Schubert's inspired setting of Goethe's poem.

319 **What He Said** Verse 40 from *Kuruntokai*, a famous anthology of ancient Tamil love poetry. 'Cempulappeyanirar' means 'poet of the red earth and pouring rain'. The verse was suggested to us by Gowri Ramnarayan, an Indian journalist who is a great fan of the Tube poems, and the poster was illustrated by her grandmother's traditional Tamil design. Supported by the Arts Council of England.

320 **The Maiden's Song** Usually anthologised as 'The Maidens Came', or sometimes 'The Bridal Morn', this charming song forms part of a narrative that describes an open-air May Day celebration in Durham, in and around the castle, in the time of Queen Elizabeth. The entire narrative, preserved in a British Library manuscript, is set to music, and includes at least one other well-known song, 'Robin, Robin [i.e. Robin Hood], Now lend thou me thy bow'. 'The bailey beareth the bell away' probably refers to the May Day games, in which the team from the castle bailey, or courtyard, carry off the prize.

322 **On a General Election** Hilaire Belloc was Liberal MP for Salford from 1906–10, and his epigram reflects his disillusionment with party politics. No doubt he felt that the Liberal Prime Minister, H. H. Asquith, was seduced by the social world introduced to him by his second wife Margot; bridge figured prominently at the country-house parties of the rich, as did champagne.

ACKNOWLEDGEMENTS

The editors and publisher gratefully acknowledge permission to reproduce the following copyright poems in this book:

Dannie Abse: 'Mysteries' from *Selected Poems*, © Dannie Abse 1994. Reprinted by permission of The Peters Fraser and Dunlop Group Limited.

Fleur Adcock: 'Immigrant' from *Selected Poems* (1983), © Fleur Adcock 1983. Reprinted by permission of Oxford University Press.

John Agard: 'Don't Call Alligator Long-Mouth till You Cross River', from *Say It Again Granny* (1986), © John Agard 1986. Reprinted by permission of Bodley Head.

Anna Akhmatova: 'Requiem' from *Selected Poems*, translation © Richard McKane 1989. Reprinted by permission of Bloodaxe Books.

Moniza Alvi: 'Arrival 1946' from *The Country at my Shoulder* (1993), © Moniza Alvi 1993. Reprinted by permission of Oxford University Press.

Maya Angelou: 'Come. And Be My Baby' from *Just Give Me A Cool Drink of Water 'Fore I Diiie*, © Maya Angelou 1971. Reprinted by permission of Virago Press.

Simon Armitage: 'The Catch' from *Kid*, © Simon Armitage 1992. Reprinted by permission of Faber and Faber.

Margaret Atwood: 'True Stories (1)' from *Collected Poems*, © Margaret Atwood 1982. Reprinted by permission of the Random House Group Ltd.

W. H. Auden: Song ('Stop all the clocks, cut off the telephone') and 'If I could tell you' from *Collected Poems* by W. H. Auden, © W. H. Auden 1968. Reprinted by permission of Faber and Faber.

Samuel Beckett: 'Fresh sighs for sale', from *Selected Poems* by Alain Bosquet (1963), translation © Calder Publications and the estate of Samuel Beckett. Reprinted by permission of Calder Publications and the estate of Samuel Beckett.

Bei Dao: 'A Picture' from *Old Snow*, Anvil, © Bei Dao 1990. Reprinted by permission of David Higham Associates.

Hilaire Belloc: 'On A General Election' from *Complete Verse*, © the Estate of Hilaire Belloc 1970. Reprinted by permission of The Peters, Fraser and Dunlop Group Ltd.

Connie Bensley: 'Shopper' from *Choosing To Be a Swan*, © Connie Bensley 1994. Reprinted by permission of Bloodaxe Books.

Gerard Benson: 'The Coming of Grendel' from *Beowulf*, and 'Old English Riddle', © Gerard Benson 1988 and 1990. Reprinted by permission of the author.

Oliver Bernard: 'Letter to André Billy. 9 April 1915' from Guillaume Apollinaire, *Selected Poems* (1986), translation © Oliver Bernard 1986.

Cicely Herbert: 'Everything Changes', © Cicely Herbert 1989. Reprinted by permission of the author. Sappho translation, © Cicely Herbert 1993. Reprinted by permission of the translator.

Geoffrey Hill: 'Merlin', from *Collected Poems* (1985), © Geoffrey Hill 1985. Reprinted by permission of Penguin Books.

Miroslav Holub: 'Spacetime' from *Vanishing Lung Syndrome*, © Miroslav Holub 1990, translation © David Young and Dana Hábová. Reprinted by permission of Faber and Faber.

Stuart Hood: 'A Collector', from *100 Poems Without a Country* (1978), translation © Stuart Hood. Reprinted by permission of Calder Publications.

A. D. Hope: 'The Gateway', from *Selected Poems* (1986), © A. D. Hope 1986. Reprinted by permission of Carcanet Press.

Langston Hughes: 'Dream Boogie' from *Selected Poems*, © Langston Hughes 1959. Reproduced by permission of David Higham Associates.

Siân Hughes: 'Secret Lives', © Siân Hughes 1996. Printed by permission of the author.

Ted Hughes: 'Full Moon and Little Frieda' from *Wodwo* by Ted Hughes, © Ted Hughes 1982. Reprinted by permission of Faber and Faber.

Paul Hyland: 'For Pero Moniz, who died at sea' from Luís de Camões, translation commissioned by Poems on the Underground © Paul Hyland 2001. Reprinted by permission of the translator.

Philippe Jaccottet: 'Les distances', from *L'Ignorant* (1957), © Philippe Jaccottet. Reprinted by permission of Editions Gallimard.

Kathleen Jamie: 'Rooms' from *The Queen of Sheba*, © Kathleen Jamie 1994. Reprinted by permission of Bloodaxe Books.

Elizabeth Jennings: 'Delay' from *Collected Poems* (1967), © Elizabeth Jennings 1986. Reprinted by permission of David Higham Associates.

Patrick Kavanagh: 'Wet Evening in April' and 'Memory of my Father' from *The Complete Poems of Patrick Kavanagh*, © Peter Kavanagh 1972, 1996. Reprinted by permission of Peter Kavanagh.

Judith Kazantzis: 'Freight song' from *Swimming Through the Grand Hotel*, © Judith Kazantzis 1997. Reprinted by permission of Enitharmon Press.

Edmund Keeley and **Philip Sherrard**: 'Longings', from *Collected Poems of C. P. Cavafy* (1990), translation © Edmund Keeley and Philip Sherrard 1975 and 1984. Reproduced by permission of the authors c/o Rogers, Coleridge & White Ltd.

X. J. Kennedy: 'To Someone Who Insisted I Look Up Someone' first appeared in *Cross Ties: Selected Poems*. Published by The University of Georgia Press. © X. J. Kennedy 1985. Reprinted by permission of Curtis Brown Ltd.

Milton Kessler: 'Thanks Forever' from *The Grand Concourse*, © Milton Kessler 1990. Reprinted by permission of the author.

Mimi Khalvati: 'Apology' from *Mirrorwork*, © Mimi Khalvati 1995. Reprinted by permission of Carcanet Press.

Stephen Knight: 'Voyage to the Bottom of the Sea' from *Flowering Limbs*,

INDEX OF POETS
AND TRANSLATORS

Abse, Dannie 186
Adcock, Fleur 48
Agard, John 236
Akhmatova, Anna 190
Alvi, Moniza 181
Angelou, Maya 121
Apollinaire, Guillaume 133, 339
Armitage, Simon 300
Arnold, Matthew 234
Atwood, Margaret 292
Auden, W. H. 80, 168, 183

Beckett, Samuel 242
Bei Dao 158–9
Belloc, Hilaire 322
Bensley, Connie 218
Benson, Gerard 71, 110
Bernard, Oliver 133, 220
Berndt, Ronald M. 301
Berry, James 34
Betjeman, John 195
Bhatt, Sujata 165
Bishop, Elizabeth 147, 283
Blake, William 35, 86–7, 268, 299
Bloom, Valerie 170
Boland, Eavan 153, 252
Bosquet, Alain 242
Bradstreet, Anne 198
Brathwaite, Kamau 103, 284
Brecht, Bertolt 306
Breeze, Jean 'Binta' 192
Breyner, Sophia de Mello 244
Brown, Clarence 106
Brown, George Mackay 205
Browning, Elizabeth Barrett 74–5
Browning, Robert 67, 260

Brutus, Dennis 217
Burns, Robert 25, 145, 276–7
Burnside, John 325
Byron, George Gordon, Lord 57, 269

Caedmon 263
Camões, Luís de 296–7
Campion, Thomas 182
Carroll, Lewis 142, 258
Causley, Charles 108, 291
Cavafy, C. P. 238
Celan, Paul 256
Cempulappeyanirar 319
Chaucer, Geoffrey 90, 265, 335
Chen Maiping 158
Chiavetta, Eleonora, 243
Chuilleanáin, Eiléan Ní 175
Clare, John 150
Clarke, Gillian 70
Coleridge, Samuel Taylor 128
Constantine, David 316
Cope, Wendy 126
Crossley-Holland, Kevin 264

D'Aguiar, Fred 231
Deane, John F. 250
de Jager, Marjolijn, 246
de la Mare, Walter 47
Dekker, Thomas 298
Dhomhnaill, Nuala Ní 237
Dickinson, Emily 36, 204, 281
Donaghy, Michael 317
Donne, John 45, 188, 288
Dooley, Maura 136
d'Orléans, Charles 220
Drayton, Michael 115

Dryden, John 199
Duffy, Carol Ann 141, 286
Dunbar, William 95

Eliot, T. S. 68
Ewart, Gavin 120

Fainlight, Ruth 76, 244
Fanthorpe, U. A. 160
Farley, Paul 262
Feinstein, Elaine 112
Fenton, James 197
Finch, see Winchilsea
Forché, Carolyn 65
Fried, Erich 245
Frost, Robert 194
Fuller, John 140

Gay, John 167
Glück, Louise 202
Goethe, J. W. von 316
Goodison, Lorna 49
Graves, Robert 113
Grieve, Christopher Murray
  see MacDiarmid, Hugh
Griffin, Jonathan 229
Gunn, Thom 235

Hábová, Dana 169
Hamburger, Michael 256
Hardy, Thomas 83
Harrison, Tony 275
Hass, Robert 93
Heaney, Seamus 28, 219, 295
Heath-Stubbs, John 152
Herbert, Cicely 89, 149
Herbert, George 111
Herrick, Robert 91, 203, 267, 345
Hill, Geoffrey 251
Holub, Miroslav 169
Hood, Stuart 245
Hope, A. D. 253
Hopkins, Gerard Manley 63, 200

Housman, A. E. 116
Hughes, Langston 151
Hughes, Siân 211
Hughes, Ted 114
Hulme, T. E. 124
Hyland, Paul 296–7

Jaccottet, Philippe 247
Jamie, Kathleen 187
Jennings, Elizabeth 88
Jonson, Ben 257

Kavanagh, Patrick 107, 210
Kazantzis, Judith 330
Keats, John 52-3, 96
Keeley, Edmund 238
Kennedy, X. J. 148
Kessler, Milton 174, 343–4
Khalvati, Mimi 207
King, Henry 233
Kipling, Rudyard 97
Knight, Stephen 232
Koltz, Anise 248

Lagerkvist, Pär 183
Langland, William 304
Larkin, Philip 33
Lawrence, D. H. 102
Lear, Edward 62
Levertov, Denise 44
Levi, Primo 243
Lim, Shirley Geok-lin 98
Lochhead, Liz 60
Logue, Christopher 69
Lomas, Herbert 206, 239
Longley, Michael 329
Lorca, Federico García 241

MacCaig, Norman 125, 315
MacDiarmid, Hugh 137
Machado, Antonio 351
McDougall, Bonnie S. 158
McGough, Roger 94

McKane, Richard 190
MacNeice, Louis 129
Mahon, Derek 64, 247
Malouf, David 308
Mandelstam, Osip 106
Marlowe, Christopher 132
Marvell, Andrew 154
Masefield, John 224
Meehan, Paula 318
Merwin, W. S. 106
Mew, Charlotte 306
Michaelis, Hanny 246
Millay, Edna St. Vincent 92, 282
Milligan, Spike 58, 185
Milosz, Czeslaw 93
Milton, John 61, 162
Mitchell, Adrian 54, 241
Montague, John 223, 248
Montale, Eugenio 328
Morgan, Edwin 43, 332–3
Muldoon, Paul 180, 237, 263
Murray, Les 164

Neruda, Pablo 209
Nichols, Grace 29, 309

O'Brien, Flann 287
Oswald, Alice 226
Owen, Wilfred 156–7

Padel, Ruth 324
Palladas 275
Parker, Dorothy 155
Paskins, Matthew 311
Paterson, Don 294
Paul, St. 278
Pessoa, Fernando 229
Pierpoint, Katherine 261
Pilkington, Laetitia 289
Plath, Sylvia 134
Pogson, Lucy 310
Pope, Alexander 221
Porter, Peter 225

Pugh, Sheenagh 131

Raine, Kathleen 146
Raleigh, Sir Walter 337–8
Ramanujan, A. K. 319
Reed, Jeremy 328
Reid, Alastair 209
Rich, Adrienne 109
Ridler, Anne 230
Rodriguez, Judith 303
Roethke, Theodore 117
Rossetti, Christina 178
Ryan, Tracy 213

Salkey, Andrew 135
Sandburg, Carl 327
Sappho 149
Sarton, May 196
Sassoon, Siegfried 42, 157
Satyamurti, Carole 82
Schwartz, Delmore 323
Senior, Olive 293
Shakespeare, William 30, 66, 171,
    208, 266, 305, 326, 340
Shapcott, Jo 274
Shelley, Percy Bysshe 26, 138–9,
    290, 339–40
Sheridan, Thomas 172
Sherrard, Philip 238
Sidney, Sir Philip 193
Sjöberg, Leif 183
Smith, Iain Crichton 191
Smith, Ken 39
Smith, Stevie 32, 271
Södergran, Edith 239
Soyinka, Wole 59, 285
Southey, Robert 307
Spender, Stephen 307
Spenser, Edmund 227
Stainer, Pauline 212
Steen, Vagn 249
Stevens, Wallace 179, 347–8
Stevenson, Anne 55, 273

Stevenson, Robert Louis 173

Tennyson, Alfred, Lord 123, 280
Thomas, Dylan 72, 184
Thomas, Edward 51, 189
Thomas, R. S. 81
Thompson, Francis 37
Tranströmer, Tomas 250
Tsvetayeva, Marina 112
Tyndale, William 278

Vaughan, Henry 313
Verlaine, Paul 223

Wakoski, Diane 104
Walcott, Derek 73, 272
Whitman, Walt 101

Wilde, Oscar 77
Williams, Hugo 201
Williams, William Carlos 27
Winchilsea, Anne Finch,
    Countess of 46
Wordsworth, William 41, 176, 279
Wright, David 130, 337
Wright, Judith 38, 302
Wright, Kit 99
Wyatt, Sir Thomas 50

Yates, Luke 312
Yeats, W. B. 31, 163, 270, 336
Young, David 169

Zhao Zhenkai *see* Bei Dao

INDEX OF FIRST LINES

	Page
$a$capitalist$	249
Adam: Lady	273
A cool small evening shrunk to a dog bark and the clank of a bucket	114
A moth, I thought, munching a word	110
A neighbourhood	252
A thing of beauty is a joy for ever	53
About ten days or so	235
Above all rivers thy river hath renown	95
Abstracted by silence from the age of seven	130
'After sharp showers,' said Peace, 'the sun shines brightest	304
All, all, of a piece throughout	199
Alles wandelt sich. Neu beginnen	348
An Oaken, broken, Elbow-Chair	172
An omnibus across the bridge	77
An' a so de rain a-fall	135
And did those feet in ancient time	268
And it was at that age . . . Poetry arrived	209
And yet the books will be there on the shelves, separate beings	93
Ann, Ann!	47
As a gale on the mountainside bends the oak tree	149
As I was walking all alane	166
At night, I do not know who I am	186
At the end of this sentence, rain will begin	272
Aunt Jennifer's tigers prance across a screen	109
Born on a sunday	231
Break my branches	248
Bright clasp of her whole hand around my finger	307
Bring me the sunflower and I'll transplant	328
Broad sun-stoned beaches	73
But no, she's abstract, is a bird	229
Call alligator long-mouth	236
Caminaute, son tus huellas	351
Cauld blaws the wind frae east to west	25

Come live with me, and be my love 132

Come, wed me, Lady Singleton 32

Dark brown is the river 173

Death be not proud, though some have called thee 45

Dicam quid sit Amor: Amor est insania mentis 340

Did anyone tell you 332

Do not go gentle into that good night 184

Don't ask for the true story 292

Drink and dance and laugh and lie 155

Drink to me only with thine eyes 257

Earth has not anything to show more fair 41

Earth in beauty dressed 31

Eastward, Mount Budawang 302

English Teeth, English Teeth! 58

Every old man I see 210

Everyone suddenly burst out singing 42

Everyone who made love the night before 201

Everything changes. We plant 89

Fear no more the heat o' the sun 305

For I have learned 279

For the present there is just one moon 317

For this, the dark, the ceasing of the winds 316

Forget 300

Found a pink wet thing 312

Fresh sighs for sale! 242

From the dull confines of the drooping West 203

From time to time our love is like a sail 226

Full fathom five thy father lies 66

Golden slumbers kiss your eyes 298

Good morning, daddy! 151

Gray goose and gander 161

Great was my joy with London at my feet 195

Gunner/Driver One (front-line) 133

Had I the heavens' embroidered cloths 163

Having a bitter on the Thames 344

369

He breathed in air, he breathed out light 54

He is a drunk leaning companionably 140

He who binds to himself a joy 299

Her first memory is of light all around her 329

Here is a glass of water from my well 196

Here we are all, by day: by night we're hurled 91

Here's a song 287

Here's fine rosemary, sage, and thyme 118

Hirsute hell chimney-spouts, black thunderthroes 59

His coomb was redder than the fyn coral 335

How do I love thee? Let me count the ways 75

How I love 324

Humming your Nocturne on the Circle Line 207

I am a poet 126

I am of Ireland 122, 336

I am spending my way out 218

I am – yet what I am none cares or knows 150

I could not dig: I dared not rob 97

I have a gentil cock 100

I have been one acquainted with the night 194

I have crossed an ocean 309

I have eaten 27

I have known the inexorable sadness of pencils 117

I know the truth – give up all other truths! 112

I live for books 104

I met a traveller from an antique land 26

I place my hope on the water 237

I rang them up while touring Timbuctoo 148

I saw a jolly hunter 108

I saw a Peacock with a fiery tail 127

I saw Eternity the other night 313

I shall say what inordinate love is 144

I sing of a maiden 255

I sing of Brooks, of Blossomes, Birds, and Bowers 267

I taste a liquor never brewed 204

I tell a wanderer's tale, the same 39

I think no longer of the antique city 291

I wanna be the leader 94

I want him to have another living summer   120
I want to drive home in the dusk   325
I want to let go   239
I will consider the outnumbering dead   251
I wish I could believe in something beyond   243
I wonder, by my troth, what thou and I   188
I would to heaven that I were so much clay   269
If all the world and love were young   338
If ever two were one, then surely we   198
I'm a strange creature, for I satisfy women   264
In drifts of sleep I came upon you   219
In either hand the hast'ning angel caught   61
In February, digging his garden, planting potatoes   136
In London   29
In my craft or sullen art   72
In Spanish he whispers there is no time left   65
'In the days of my youth,' Father William replied   350
In the gloom of whiteness   51
In the middle of the sporting green   223
Into my heart an air that kills   116
It is little I repair to the matches of the Southron folk   37
It was her voice that made   347

Know then thyself, presume not God to scan   221

Labour is blossoming or dancing where   270
Last night I dreamt in Chinese   98
Last night in London Airport   69
Legs I have got, yet seldom do I walk   314
Let me not to the marriage of true minds   266
Let my shadow disappear into yours   183
Like oil lamps we put them out the back   153
Like the beautiful bodies of those who died before growing old   238
Like to the falling of a star   233
Look at all those monkeys   185
Look at those empty ships   174
Love holds me captive again   149
Love without hope, as when the young bird-catcher   113
Loving the rituals that keep men close   275
Lying is an occupation   289

Mad in pursuit, and in possession so   340
Many policemen wear upon their shoulders   99
Margaret, are you grieving   63
Mars is braw in crammasy   137
More discontents I never had   345
Morning arrives in a sleeveless dress   158
Much have I travell'd in the realms of gold   96
Much Madness is divinest Sense   36
Music, when soft voices die   139
My beloved spake, and said unto me, Rise up, my love, my fair one,
    and come away   105
My candle burns at both ends   282
My first is in life (not contained within heart)   60
My heart is like a singing bird   178
My love is faren in a land   214
My mother's old leather handbag   76
My true love hath my heart and I have his   193

No man is an island, entire of itself; every man is a piece of
    the continent, a part of the main   288
Nobody heard him, the dead man   271
Not knowing even that we're on the way   160
November '63: eight months in London   48
Now from the marshlands under the mist-mountains   71
Now sleeps the crimson petal, now the white   123
Now the heart sings with all its thousand voices   253
Now we must praise to the skies the Keeper of the
    heavenly kingdom   263
Now welcome Summer with thy sunnė soft   90
Now winter nights enlarge   182

O my Luve's like a red, red rose   145
O roving Muse, recall that wondrous year   167
O Rose thou art sick   35
Oh, to be in England   260
On earth I lived few years, and weary ones   296
Once, in finesse of fiddles found I ecstasy   124
Only a man harrowing clods   83
Our mothers have a thing   293

Peaceful waters of the air   241
Pile the bodies high at Austerlitz and Waterloo   327
Premier cannonier conducteur   339
Propped against the crowded bar   284

Quinquireme of Nineveh from distant Ophir   224

Rain here on a tableau of cows   225
Rain on lilac leaves. In the dusk   70
Rain rains at half one in the morning and   310
Ring out, wild bells, to the wild sky   280
Ropey, lippy, loopy, scribbly   303
Rust is ripeness, rust   285

Shall I compare thee to a summer's day?   171
Ships reflected on the waves   311
Should auld acquaintance be forgot   276
Since there's no help, come let us kiss and part   115
Sleep well, my love, sleep well   217
So we'll go no more a-roving   57
Softly, in the dusk, a woman is singing to me   102
Some days, although we cannot pray, a prayer   286
Some verses, written when he was alive   337
sometimes   192
Sometimes things don't go, after all   131
Sometimes your dressing gown unhooks   211
Somewhere in the house   246
Somewhere on the other side of this wide night   141
Spring's come, a little late, in the park   206
Sssnnnwhuffl?   43
Stop all the clocks, cut off the telephone   80
Such days, when trees run downwind   315
Sumer is icumen in   79
Summer is over upon the sea   283
Summon now the kings of the forest   103
Sun a-shine an' rain a-fall   170
Sweet day, so cool, so calm, so bright   111
Sweet Spirit! Sister of that orphan one   339
Swifts turn in the heights of the air   247
Tagus farewell, that westward with thy streams   50

Thanks to the ear   34
That time of year thou mayst in me behold   326
The accursèd power which stands on Privilege   322
The art of losing isn't hard to master   147
The birds sang in the wet trees   107
The boat docked in at Liverpool   181
The candid freezing season again   230
The darkness lifts, imagine, in your lifetime   202
The day breaks – the first rays of the rising Sun, stretching her arms   301
The fire in leaf and grass   44
The first warm day of spring   318
The forest drips and glows with green   38
The Frost performs its secret ministry   128
The goddess Fortune be praised (on her toothed wheel)   152
The grey sea and the long black land   67
The highway is full of big cars   121
The hour of remembrance has drawn close again   190
The houses are haunted   179
The many ships that left our country   191
The mind is a city like London   323
The moon falls   212
The paddocks shave black   164
The radiance of that star that leans on me   88
The railway station in winter lies wide open on three sides   261
The room was suddenly rich and the great bay-window was   129
The salmon lying in the depths of Llyn Llifon   81
The sea is calm tonight   234
The season midnight: glass   308
The silver swan, who living had no note   56
The small schoolgirl   213
The things I found   245
The trees are coming into leaf   33
The trick (he tells me) is to sleep till twelve   232
The very leaves of the acacia-tree are London   146
The weather's cast its cloak of grey   220
The winter evening settles down   68
The world is too much with us; late and soon   176
The world's great age begins anew   290
Then a powerful demon, a prowler through the dark   295

Then came the *Autumne* all in yellow clad 227
There came a Wind like a Bugle 281
There was an Old Man with a beard 62
There were three Ravens sat on a tree 342
Therefore he no more troubled the pool of silence 205
They won't let railways alone, those yellow flowers 55
This dárksome búrn, hórseback brówn 200
This is the dawn I was waiting for 244
This is the wind, the wind in a field of corn 197
Though I love this travelling life and yearn 187
Thread suns 256
Tide be runnin' the great world over 306
Time will say nothing but I told you so 168
Tired of all who come with words, words but no language 250
Trail all your pikes, dispirit every drum 46
'Transcendental,' said the technician 274
Traveller, your footprints are 294
Trees are cages for them: water holds its breath 125
Two sticks and an apple 84
Two women, seventies, hold hands 82
Tyger Tyger, burning bright 87

Under the greenwood tree 208

We sat like slum landlords around the board 262
We were lying, the two of us 330
Western wind when wilt thou blow 40
Whan that Aprill with his shoures soote 265
What am I after all but a child, pleas'd with the sound of my own
    name? repeating it over and over 101
What could my mother be 319
What lips my lips have kissed, and where, and why 92
What passing-bells for these who die as cattle? 156
What profit hath a man of all his labour which he taketh under
    the sun? 216
What wondrous life in this I lead! 154
When all this is over, said the swineherd 175
When I am sad and weary 54
When I consider how my light is spent 162

When I grow up and you get small   169
When I was a child, I spake as a child, I understood   278
When I was in my mother's bower   320
When in disgrace with Fortune and men's eyes   30
When we climbed the slopes of the cutting   28
'When you stop to consider   64
'Will you walk a little faster?' said a whiting to a snail   142

Years later we'll remember the bathtub   165
Yellow/brown woman   49
Yes. I remember Adlestrop   189
'You are old, father William,' the young man said   258
You remember that village where the border ran   180
You took away all the oceans and all the room   106
Your clear eye is the one absolutely beautiful thing   134

A NOTE OF THANKS

'POEMS ON THE UNDERGROUND' depends on the cooperation and support of London Underground, which provides advertising spaces free of charge and pays the production costs of the programme. We are also grateful for generous financial support from London Arts, the Arts Council of England, the Calouste Gulbenkian Foundation and the British Council, which displays the Tube posters in its libraries and offices abroad. We would also like to thank Tom Davidson, who has designed the posters since 1989 with clarity and elegance.

Many organisations have sponsored specific projects over the years, including special commissions, poetry competitions, concerts and readings. Chief among these have been the British Library, the National Portrait Gallery, the Department for Culture, Media and Sport, Visiting Arts, *The Times Literary Supplement*, the British Tourist Authority, the National Year of Reading, the Australian Tourist Commission, the Cañada Blanch Foundation, BT affiliate Syntegra and, most recently, the Goethe Institute and the Italian Cultural Centre, supporting the inclusion of European poetry in our programme.

We have received unfailing assistance from the Librarians and staff of the British Library, the Poetry Library (South Bank Centre), the Northern Poetry Library, the Barbican Library and the University of London Library, which held an exhibition about our project in the summer of 1998.

The number of friends and colleagues who have given encouragement and practical advice is too great to list here – to all, our thanks. But we must single out our editor (and friend) at Cassell, Barry Holmes, whose tact and humour have kept our anthology afloat through good times and bad.

Readers may like to know that copies of the Underground poem posters can be purchased from the London Transport Museum, Covent Garden, and the Poetry Society.